Research Issues
in Health and Social Care

Other Health & Social Care books from M&K include:

Routine Blood Results Explained 2/e
ISBN: 978-1-905539-38-3 · 2007

Pre-Teen and Teenage Pregnancy:
A 21st century reality
ISBN: 978-1-905539-11-6 · 2007

The Management of COPD in Primary and Secondary Care
ISBN: 978-1-905539-28-4 · 2007

The Clinician's Guide to Chronic Disease Management
for Long Term Conditions:
A cognitive-behavioural approach
ISBN: 978-1-905539-15-4 · 2008

The ECG Workbook
ISBN: 978-1-905539-14-7 · 2008

Identification and Treatment of Alcohol Dependency
ISBN: 978-1-905539-16-1 · 2008

Managing Emotions in Women's Health
ISBN: 978-1-905539-07-9 · Forthcoming 2009

Living with Dying:
Perspectives on death, dying and living with loss
ISBN: 978-1-905539-21-5 · Forthcoming 2009

Research Issues in Health and Social Care

Dr David Cowan

Research Issues in Health and Social Care
David Cowan

ISBN: 978-1-905539-20-8

First published 2009

British Library Catalogue in Publication Data
A catalogue record for this book is available from the British Library

Notice
Clinical practice and medical knowledge constantly evolve. Standard safety precautions must be followed, but, as knowledge is broadened by research, changes in practice, treatment and drug therapy may become necessary or appropriate. Readers must check the most current product information provided by the manufacturer of each drug to be administered and verify the dosages and correct administration, as well as contraindications. It is the responsibility of the practitioner, utilising the experience and knowledge of the patient, to determine dosages and the best treatment for each individual patient. Any brands mentioned in this book are as examples only and are not endorsed by the Publisher. Neither the publisher nor the authors assume any liability for any injury and/or damage to persons or property arising from this publication.

The Publisher

To contact M&K Publishing write to:
M&K Update Ltd · The Old Bakery · St. John's Street
Keswick · Cumbria CA12 5AS

Tel: 01768 773030 · Fax: 01768 781099
publishing@mkupdate.co.uk
www.mkupdate.co.uk

Designed and typeset in 11pt Usherwood Book by Mary Blood
Printed in England by Ferguson Print, Keswick.

Contents

List of tables

Introduction

This book is aimed at various health and social care practitioners including: nurses, midwives, doctors, social workers, health promotion and public health practitioners, health visitors and hospital managers, and in particular, those who are studying a multidisciplinary research course. There appears to be no single book on the topic of general research issues that is relevant to all of the above. This lack has resulted in requests from a diverse range of research students for the development of a suitable textbook. Thus, the book is intended to complement a multidisciplinary research course or indeed, any other type of research endeavour such as a dissertation. Furthermore, the book should be of general use to anybody studying health and/or social care research at undergraduate or postgraduate level.

The aim is to impart information on research issues to a diverse range of health and social care practitioners in a way that is meaningful, drawing on examples and material that has relevance to practice settings.

In the contemporary climate where emphasis is on multidisciplinary working and evidence-based practice in health and social care, there is indeed a need for a book whose focus is not restricted to either health care or social care approaches to research. (In fact very few books on research for social workers exist anyway.) In particular, subsequent to increasing convergence of various areas of health care and social care practice, such a book would facilitate exploitation of the potential for multidisciplinary based research to inform evidence-based practice. These areas of convergence include: organisational change, service delivery, leadership, service user involvement, general care in the community, care of physically disabled people, care of older people, child protection, problematic use of drugs and alcohol, sexual abuse, sexual health, sex education, domestic violence, mental health, medication management and nutrition management.

In addition, it is intended that this book will ameliorate some of the problems encountered by research students due to confusion caused by the ambiguous use of research terminology.

Indeed, in order to address some of the ambiguity in the use of various research terms, throughout the book there will be a series of 'Terminology Boxes'.

Research issues in health and social care

In addition to the above reasons, this book may also be of interest to anybody who is becoming increasingly perplexed by the amount of health and social care orientated research information that we are bombarded with in contemporary society. This is not just information which is directly pertinent to health and social care practice, but also that which is ancillary, such as reports in the media on diets, lifestyle, alcohol consumption, recreational drug use, health products and statistics on numerous health and social issues including crime and various health and fitness regimes. All of these issues are now underpinned to varying degrees by research, this research being of varying robustness. In reading this book and understanding various research issues in greater depth and in acquiring some critical appraisal skills, it should then be possible to examine the strengths and weaknesses of different types of research evidence.

Accordingly, this book can be used as an aid to formal study or can be used as an aid to further understanding health and social care research issues for reasons of personal interest. In either case, the book can be read 'cover to cover' or more likely, be 'dipped into' depending on the specific area or issue of interest.

Chapter 1
Knowledge and uncertainty

Introduction

Research is inextricably connected with knowledge. Indeed, research is often used as a way of creating new knowledge, building upon existing knowledge and closing perceived knowledge gaps. This applies to many disciplines, including those of health and social care. Conversely though, while research may inform knowledge, the opposite is also true – approaches to research are in turn informed and underpinned by different knowledge constructs.

This chapter invites the reader to begin contemplating, exploring and questioning certain assumptions about what constitutes knowledge and how such knowledge is generated, applied and perceived. This can be described as an epistemological process. Epistemology is the theory of knowledge, derived from the Greek words *episteme* (knowledge or science) and *logos* (account or explanation) and is concerned with studying the conditions, the limits and validity of what we know, or what we think we know. Much of the debate in the field of epistemology has focused on analysing the nature of knowledge and how it relates to notions such as truth and belief. It also deals with the means of producing knowledge, as well as scepticism about different knowledge claims. Thus, epistemology primarily addresses the following questions:

- What is knowledge?
- How is knowledge acquired?
- How much can people know?

However, it can be suggested that this discourse is not complete without the inclusion of what can be seen as the antithesis of knowledge, namely, uncertainty. Indeed, there are still many uncertainties in health and social care practice which appear to be informed more through intuition or 'rule of thumb' rather than by research-generated, evidence-based decision making.

In order to trace and examine the origins of contemporary knowledge construction and philosophical approaches to it, we will begin with a brief journey back through time. In doing so, you will be introduced to some of the philosophers and thinkers, who, throughout recent centuries, have influenced intellectual thought, reasoning, knowledge construction and scientific development.

The Renaissance

The Renaissance

Following the social turmoil caused throughout Europe by the bubonic plague epidemic of the late 14th century, people started to contemplate existential issues differently (Rawcliffe 1995). Faith in a divine saviour and confidence in the effectiveness of medical interventions were severely tested. Illustrative of this, many of those who were perceived to have a 'direct line' to the Almighty, namely the clergy, were as helpless in the wake of the 'Black Death' as the rest of the population and were struck down with equal regularity and devastation. This was equally true of many of the medical 'experts' of the time. Thus, during the 15th century, certain philosophers began to question the perceived 'fact' that there was a 'natural order' controlling human life which could not be subject to change by mere mortals. Indeed, the 15th century Renaissance is perceived by many as marking the beginning of what can be generally termed the 'Modern Period' which culminated in what came to be known as the 'Age of Reason' (also known as the Age of Rationalism), the 'Age of Enlightenment' and the subsequent emergence of modern societies and modern science.

Depending on what one reads in various publications on the Modern Period and on one's own perspective, the 'Age of Enlightenment' may include the earlier period (the Age of Reason), or can comprise only the period directly after. For the purposes of this commentary, the latter definition applies whereby the Age of Reason and the Age of Enlightenment are seen as separate parts of the Modern Period. Regardless, the new ideas and ways of thinking that emerged during this time replaced the knowledge systems that had prevailed in Britain and Europe for centuries. Thus, 'divine' knowledge that was 'revealed' via theological sources and knowledge of the supernatural, based on unfounded superstition, was gradually replaced by scientific knowledge, this being manufactured by humans. Furthermore, the Renaissance was characterised by the beginning of reconnection of Western European thinking with the philosophies and teachings of classical antiquity, particularly that of the ancient Greeks. There was renewed interest in mathematics, complemented by the creation of new techniques in architecture and the arts. This was facilitated further by a significant increase in the distribution of information facilitated by the important invention of the printing press.

One of the most significant commentators of the time was the German/Polish (there is dispute over his true nationality (Allgemeine Deutsche Biographie 1912)) astronomer, mathematician and physician Nicolaus Copernicus (1473–1543). In his thesis 'On the Revolutions of the Celestial Spheres', Copernicus proposed that the sun rather than the earth was at the centre of the then known universe. His heliocentric (sun-centred) theory is considered to be one of the most important scientific theories in history. It signified the start of the shift away from the theological model of knowledge construction, the beginning of modern astronomy and subsequently, modern science.

Illustrative of the abovementioned reconnection with the ancient Greeks, in support of his theory, Copernicus cited the earlier work of astronomers and philosophers in the 3rd and 4th centuries, namely Aristarchus and Philolaus. However, since Copernicus' theory contradicted the Old Testament account of the sun's movement around the earth (Joshua 10:13), it is likely that Copernicus was wary of incurring the wrath of the religious authorities in Rome (Rosen 1995). Thus, Copernicus' book was published with a preface by a respected Lutheran theologian, stating that the heliocentric theory was a mere mathematical model, which may not actually hold any truth or likelihood (Rosen 1995).

The Age of Reason

**The Age of
Reason**

As mentioned, at the beginning of the 17th century the Renaissance period was succeeded by the 'Age of Reason' which, can be seen as the forerunner to the 'Age of Enlightenment'. It was during the Age of Reason that the idea of intellectual enquiry gained popularity and philosophers began to question further still the concept of the existence of divine eternal facts or 'truths' as disseminated through the teachings of the Roman Catholic Church (Smith 1998). One such philosopher was the Italian physicist Galileo Galilei (1564–1642). Galileo's achievements include a description of the first and second laws of motion, improvements to the telescope and subsequently a series of improved astronomical observations, which led him to support Copernicus' heliocentric model of the solar system.

However, bearing out the concerns of Copernicus in the previous century, in 1633, at nearly 70 years of age, Galileo was put on trial for heresy before the Holy Inquisition, resulting in him denouncing his own work in order to avoid the death penalty (Sharratt 1996). Despite this, Galileo's work and his conflict with the religious authorities can be seen as representative of the widening conflict between the Church and scientific freedom of thought in Western society which culminated in what became known as the 'Scientific Revolution' (Smith 1998).

Other contemporary philosophers had been arriving at similar conclusions with regard to the importance of observation. In England, the philosopher Francis Bacon became a prominent advocate and defender of the Scientific Revolution. Bacon, a great admirer of Galileo, proposed the theory of observation and experimentation, which marked the beginning of what became known as the 'Empiricist' doctrine, which continues to this day to influence the way modern science is conducted (Urbach 1987). Bacon advocated doing away with the idea of 'a priori' speculation (speculation prior to, or independent of, experience) as a source of knowledge about the world, and emphasised the importance of 'a posteriori' theorising (theory based on experience). Thus, the Baconian method of enquiry as it became known, relied upon knowledge based on the new methods derived from observation and experiment as opposed to being based merely on pure thought (Urbach 1987). This also became popularly known as the 'inductive' method of constructing knowledge (Urbach 1987). Bacon reasoned that through the process of induction it was possible to construct scientific knowledge through the discovery of 'forms', these being the structures and ways in which natural phenomena occur and their origins (Urbach 1987). Bacon argued that through induction and through breaking objects down to their smallest possible parts to understand their workings, scientists could discover the truth and in this way could demystify false and irrational interpretations of the world, as the truth was often obscured by delusions which he referred to as 'idols' (Smith 1998, Urbach 1987).

Mindful of the dangers of appearing to question matters of divine faith, by focusing on the scientific experimental method, Bacon managed to avoid antagonising the religious authorities. In this way, Bacon suggested that subsequent to observations from within a specific context or set of conditions it could be left to the individual to decide on the robustness of ensuing evidence (Urbach 1987). Bacon met with considerable difficulty in convincing contemporary academics, many of whom were in universities controlled by the Church, of the notion that truth might be determined by scientific observation rather than the divine power of God. Despite this, Bacon's inductive approach eventually revolutionised the future thinking process of humanity (Urbach 1987). However, it should be noted that in contemporary research terms, the process of induction is now used to refer to the process of inducing or generating theories, as opposed to generating truths. This matter will be returned to later in this book.

Rationalism

Rationalism

Another important philosopher of the period was the French mathematician and scientist Rene Descartes (1596–1650). Descartes can be regarded as the founder of modern philosophy and mathematics (Smith 1998). It was Descartes who provided the first philosophical framework for the natural sciences. Descartes advocated that consciousness was the starting point for rationality (reason) this being the only reliable method for attaining knowledge (Clarke 2006). However, while realising that real things could be perceived through the senses, Descartes acknowledged that these same senses could be deceptive. Thus, Descartes developed a system of knowledge construction which became known as Rationalism, discarding mere perception as unreliable and recognising 'deduction' as a method for determining the truth (Clarke 2006). In his work 'Discourse on Method', Descartes established the four 'Laws of the Cartesian Method' as follows:

- To accept nothing as true that is not recognised by reason as clear and distinct
- To analyse complex ideas by breaking them down into their simple constitutive elements, which reason can then intuitively apprehend
- To reconstruct, beginning with simple ideas and working towards the complex
- To make an accurate and complete enumeration of the data of the problem, using in this step both the methods of induction and deduction.

Thus, according to Descartes, from a starting point of clear and distinct ideas, logically progressing from one step to the next, we will arrive at truths which are all clear and distinct, because all participate in the same degree of truth enjoyed by the first idea, which was clear and distinct (Clarke 2006). Thus, Descartes reasoned that whatever can be known must be verified through rational (reasoned) objectivity and that judgements based purely on values did not constitute knowledge and therefore did not belong in the realm of science (Clarke 2006). In this way, Descartes transferred the reasoning of mathematics to philosophy, with the intention of starting with clear and distinct ideas, and of deducing from these, through reason alone, an entire system of truths which would also be real or objective.

It should be noted though that as with the contemporary application of the term 'induction', with regard to research, the term 'deduction' is now largely associated with testing theories or hypotheses, as opposed to deducing 'truths'. Induction, deduction and hypotheses will be returned to in Chapter 3 on developing a research question.

Subsequently, in contemplating ontological proof of the

existence of God, which was prone to the same doubt as his potentially deceptive perceptions, Descartes established the possibility of acquiring knowledge based on a synthesis of deduction and perception. However, Descartes also made the important distinction between mind and body, which marked the beginning of professional disciplines such as anatomy and physiology, psychology and psychiatry (Clarke 2006). This also marked the beginning of the shift away from the ancient yet predominant 'humoral theory' of employing a holistic approach to mental and physical ailments, based on treating imbalances in the bodily humours of black bile, yellow bile, phlegm and blood. (Humoral theory will be returned to in the following chapter on evidence-based practice.)

Empiricism

Empiricism

While Cartesian Rationalism, or Continental Rationalism as it was known, was predominant in Continental Europe, in Britain, the philosophical approach of 'Empiricism' was predominant. Empiricism, derived from the Greek word *empeiria*, meaning experience, is based on the need for experience in the construction of knowledge and denial that knowledge can be obtained through 'a priori' (prior) speculation.

Once again, this approach reflects a reconnection with the ancient Greeks, as Aristotle can be classified as an early Empiricist given that he and his contemporaries advocated the use and value of practical experience and observation in the rigorous study of health and disease (Open University 1991). While Bacon is credited with the observation and experimentation approach that signified the origins of contemporary empiricism, the English philosopher, doctor of medicine and politician, John Locke (1632–1704) is credited with founding the school of empirical thought (Dunn 1984).

Locke's work *An Essay Concerning Human Understanding* (1690) can be seen as the basis for the 18th century 'Enlightenment' and was concerned with determining the limits of human understanding with regard to God, the self, natural phenomena and ultimately the epistemological issue of what can legitimately claim to be known and what cannot be known. Despite his acceptance of the existence of God, Locke did not consider man to be a creature that entered this world with fixed ideas. According to Locke there was no such thing as an innate idea, no such thing as a moral precept and we are born with an empty mind which is 'a blank tablet', ready to be 'written on' by sensory experience. Thus, beginning empty, the human mind acquires knowledge through the use of the five senses and the process of reflection (Dunn 1984).

Much of Locke's work was characterised by his opposition to superstition and authoritarianism, these linked through the power of the religious authorities (Dunn 1984). Locke attacked metaphysical arguments which proposed that certain objects, such as the soul, could not be directly observed and claimed that such objects cannot be said to exist (Smith 1998). Like Descartes, Locke argued that we should use reason to search for truth rather than unquestioningly accept the word of the Church or Government. As a consequence of his opposition to the divine right of Kings and the Roman Catholic religion favoured by the English monarchy, in 1683 Locke went into exile in Holland. Following the accession to the English throne of William of Orange, Locke returned to England where he was appointed to the Board of Trade. Many of Locke's political ideas such as those relating to property rights, natural justice and Government's duty to protect these, were later embodied in the constitution of the United States of America. While Locke's Empiricism with its doctrine of experimental science has continued to dominate, it should be noted that Locke also advocated that knowledge construction, such as belief in the existence of God, could be through reasoning and intuition, these being traits of Rationalism.

A contemporary of Locke was Sir Isaac Newton (1643–1727), the English physicist, mathematician, astronomer, philosopher and Member of Parliament. Newton's mathematical calculations changed the way the universe is understood and he was the first to demonstrate that the motion of objects on Earth and celestial bodies are governed by the same set of natural laws. This was central to the Scientific Revolution and the advancement of the heliocentric model of the solar system, as Newton demonstrated that planets were held in place by the gravity of the sun (Smith

1998). Newton's *Philosophiae Naturalis Principia Mathematica* (1803, originally published 1687) described universal gravitation. Newton's three laws of motion are the basis for classical mechanics, which explain how objects move when a force is exerted upon them and that gravity is the force of attraction between two objects. Newton developed an empirical law of cooling, discovered the spectrum of colours in light, studied the speed of sound and proposed a theory for the origin of the stars. He also can claim part of the credit for the development of modern calculus (Tiner 1975).

Terminology box

Empiricism

- Knowledge is derived only from that which can be perceived through the human senses – primarily through observation and experimentation.

- Knowledge cannot be obtained through 'a priori' (prior) speculation.

- Experienced and observed phenomena lead to propositions that attempt explanation.

- Propositions may be tested through experiment.

The Age of Enlightenment

The Age of Enlightenment

While the 17th century in Britain and Europe marked increasing detachment of philosophical thinking from theological doctrine, throughout the 18th century 'Age of Enlightenment', so named because it contrasted with the preceding 'Dark Ages', philosophers continued to be inspired by the new methods proposed by Bacon, Descartes and Locke. They were inspired further by new scientific laws and regularities, such as those proposed by Newton, and it was speculated that the same 'objective truths' could be applied to any human activity and the world could be guided to future progress, escaping the Dark Ages, which had been typified by doubt, superstition, tyranny and irrationality.

Research issues in health and social care

These intellectuals now represented the emergence of a 'secular intelligentsia', capable, for the first time, of directly challenging the religious authorities (Smith 1998). Consequently, social transformation began to take place as scientists and researchers began to build upon and develop new knowledge systems in order to discover objective truths and scientific facts. This challenge is illustrated in the words of the German philosopher Immanuel Kant (1724–1804): 'have the courage to use your own understanding', which became something of a slogan for the Enlightenment (Smith 1998). However, it may be argued that if a single piece of work epitomises the Enlightenment, it is the 'Encyclopedie' published in France between 1751 and 1772 (Smith 1998). The driving force behind this work was Denis Diderot (1713–1784) who, along with other 'philosophes' as they were known, directly challenged the authority of the Catholic Church. They proposed that knowledge based directly on experience and that which was derived from experiments such as Newton's was far superior to knowledge based on intuition or faith (Havens 1955). The philosophes advocated that the universe should not be perceived as a mysterious place and that it was, like human beings, susceptible to methodological, rational investigation (Havens 1955, Smith 1998).

However, the philosophes' interests were broader than the study of philosophy and astronomy and they believed that the supremacy of scientific knowledge could be applied to medicine, the economy, law, psychology and to the study of social issues. Thus, progressing further from Descartes' mind and body dichotomy, the professionalisation of knowledge accelerated, which in turn accelerated the disciplinary specialisation of particular fields of study such as was exemplified by the increasing professionalisation of medicine (Smith 1998).

Thus the philosophes sought to combine belief in the new scientific method with anti-religious sentiment and at times, anti-authoritarian, anti-monarchist, republican views. In this way, they sought to reduce social inequalities through the progress of truth and humanitarianism (Smith 1998).

Within the Enlightenment movement there were two broad schools of philosophical thought. One was the 'Continental

Knowledge and uncertainty

Enlightenment' and the other the 'British Enlightenment'. While the former embodied the ethos of knowledge derived from Rationalism (or reason) and was influenced by earlier thinkers such as Descartes, the latter embodied that of knowledge based on Locke's Empiricism, that is, knowledge derived from experience and observation. Further to this, there was belief that combined with observation there should be a healthy sense of doubt with regard to how accurately objective truths could be identified (Smith 1998).

One of the main proponents of this empirical scepticism was the Scottish philosopher, economist and historian, David Hume (1711–1776). Hume proposed that even empiricists, in search of facts, were susceptible to allowing themselves to be influenced by their own habitual ideas and values, such as moral beliefs (Kemp Smith 1941). Hume argued that if a relationship between two variables was observed in a particular situation, that it cannot be assumed that this relationship will be observed in another situation. Also, that it was not possible to infer which variable represents the cause or which variable represents the effect of a particular reaction (Kemp Smith 1941).

Hume advocated that those citing the scientific method in search of truth should limit themselves to claiming that a particular relationship had been demonstrated, in that this had been empirically observed across time (Smith 1998). Furthermore, scientists should always maintain a healthy sense of doubt and recognise a degree of uncertainty when attempting an explanation based on the probability and predictability of an event (Smith 1998). Locke's and subsequently Hume's logic would come to underpin the philosophical approach which can be broadly termed as positivism, which will be discussed below.

In the meantime, Hume, who had expounded further on Locke's dislike of the metaphysical and dismissed as mere illusion any supernatural phenomena that could not be properly substantiated, like Galileo, also found himself in trouble with the religious authorities. Hume narrowly avoided being convicted of heresy and is likely to have been passed over for several senior academic positions due to his atheism.

While the philosophical approaches of Empiricism and

Rationalism can be contrasted, broadly speaking, these views are not mutually exclusive, since it is possible to be both empiricist and rationalist. Indeed, Immanuel Kant, who had studied Rationalism in Germany, but was also influenced by Newtonian mathematical physics and Humean scepticism, advocated that there was a middle ground where the two approaches of Empiricism and Rationalism met (Broad 1978). In his *Critique of Pure Reason* (1781–1787) Kant proposed that reason and observation operate in unison when imaginative constructions of the mind are used to organise experience (Broad 1978). Thus, observations, perceptions and impressions only make sense to us when situated within a mental framework (Smith 1998).

Positivism

Positivism

Influenced by Empiricism and the experiments of Newton which were able to test hypotheses, the French philosopher Auguste Comte (1798–1857) developed a secular movement known as positivism. This according to Comte was to counter the undue influences of the supernatural and metaphysical approaches to knowledge creation (Smith 1998). Positivism placed emphasis on reason and logic and was so named because the approach to knowledge creation was deemed to be positive in the sense that it offered an objective and true account of nature and society (Smith 1998).

Comte divided the progress of mankind into three historical stages:

1. Theological, which relies on supernatural agencies to explain what man cannot otherwise explain
2. Metaphysical, whereby man attributes effects to abstract but poorly understood causes
3. Positive, whereby man now understands the scientific laws which control the world.

Comte is also credited with founding the social sciences and believed that human behaviour would obey laws just as strict as those proposed by Newton (Smith 1998). Further, if these laws could be discovered, then social and moral evils could be eliminated, much in the same way that medical scientists were discovering disease causation and were eliminating some of the suffering which had traditionally represented an integral part of the human condition (Smith 1998). Positivists made a number of assumptions. They advocated that the methods of studying the natural sciences could be transferred to the social sciences, that if something cannot be experienced by our physical senses it is metaphysical and therefore cannot be said to exist, that concepts that cannot be experienced are meaningless, that objects of scientific study should be broken down into their smallest constituent parts, that scientific laws can be generated from statements of empirical regularities, that facts (which can be empirically verified) could be separated from values and that only facts can be regarded as scientific (Smith 1998).

Thus, positivist scientists, having preference for empirical data, based on that which can be observed, measured, replicated and quantified, believed that law-like regularities could be generated from this quantitative evidence and then used to provide explanations which could be generalised to similar situations and to predict future events in such situations (Smith 1998).

However, when Comte, succumbing to mental illness, proclaimed that positivism was a new religion, the positivist ethos became increasingly criticised and was subject to a number of challenges and modifications (Smith 1998). Having said that, some fundamental aspects of positivism still exist in various forms, as will be discussed in more detail in Chapter 4 on quantitative research methods.

Uncertainty

Uncertainty

Despite the undoubted progress that was made, the legacy of the Enlightenment still presents us with a degree of contradiction and uncertainty. On the one hand, it was advocated that humans can generate knowledge in the form of objective truths in order to determine what is certain or factual, yet on the other hand, in the spirit of critical enquiry, existing knowledge and preconceived ideas must be continually questioned and challenged and therefore, by definition must be deemed as uncertain.

Research issues in health and social care

So far, we have seen a chronological representation of how medieval, pre-modern knowledge construction was transformed through the ages and replaced by knowledge based on 'modernism'. However, while scientific progress, both in the natural sciences, which study natural phenomena and in the social sciences, which study human behaviour and societies, has advanced considerably, we still live in an age of relative uncertainty. Some of the origins of this uncertainty can be traced back to the Enlightenment and the centuries immediately preceding it.

While the philosophical approaches of Rationalism and Empiricism can be contrasted, it can also be seen that they are not mutually exclusive, as, in the case of Locke, it is possible to be both. Indeed, as noted, Kant proposed that reason and observation operate in unison to organise experience (Broad 1978). However, it is apparent that a dualism exists between Empiricism, whereby emphasis is placed on knowledge being generated through experience, observation and experimentation, and Rationalism whereby emphasis is placed on knowledge being founded on reasoning, which by definition must be 'a priori' and independent of experience. While in conciliation, Kant proposes that we need to do both in order to construct knowledge, it is apparent that the dualism between 'true' knowledge and uncertainty remains and that there are further dichotomies underpinning this dualism, such as Locke's claim that we are all born with no innate properties, versus counter claims that we all have innate intrinsic characteristics.

At issue then is the fundamental source of human knowledge and the appropriate techniques for verifying what we know or think we know, this being, as already mentioned at the beginning of this chapter, an essentially epistemological question. In trying to answer this, it may be helpful to view the following dichotomies as themes, many of which will recur throughout this book and indeed throughout life in general.

Dichotomies

Dichotomies

- objective versus subjective
- innate (intrinsic, internal) versus learned (extrinsic, external)
- fact versus value
- quantitative versus qualitative
- cause versus effect
- science versus culture
- evidence versus belief/opinion.

It should be borne in mind that the above list is not intended to be exhaustive or 'written in stone' and that the reader is invited to question it and to formulate some of their own dichotomies. To exemplify the uncertain aspects of human knowledge further, it may be helpful to examine some of the above dichotomies in more detail in order to demonstrate how they may relate to everyday perceptions.

First of all, with regard to objective versus subjective, we may ask whether or not objective knowledge is truly detached from any subjectivity. In the natural sciences it is usually assumed that objects of analysis, such as DNA, are separate from the researcher (Smith 1998). Regardless of how the researcher might 'feel' towards or value a piece of DNA, this will not alter the structure – (unless of course the DNA is tampered with). So, it may be reasonable to assume that a piece of DNA can be studied in a fairly detached, objective way.

However, how detached from everyday life can or should other types of research be? This is particularly so in the social sciences. The dilemma remains of how to bridge the gap between detached scientific knowledge and the human existence or relationships that such knowledge seeks to represent or explain. In the search for objective scientific laws and hard facts we could reject everyday experience as irrelevant or, alternatively we can embrace this in order to gain insights into aspects of social existence which would otherwise remain unnoticed. Another dimension of the objective/subjective problem is that when we study social constructs such as culture or the family, we are very often a part of our own object of analysis.

With regard to innate (intrinsic, internal) versus learned

(extrinsic, external), we could contemplate how we know what, or who we are. For example, do we know why we like what we like? Do we know why humans are attracted to members of the opposite sex – or indeed in some cases the same sex? Is this attraction innate, an intrinsic property of ourselves? Were we born this way or were we born with Locke's proposed empty mind and was it something we learned, an extrinsic property of the world, that moulded us in this way during life's experiences?

Indeed, we can ask whether it was nature or nurture that influenced us, or both? Interestingly, up until 1973, the American Psychiatric Association classified homosexuality as a disease (Schaler 2000). So, with regard to the fact versus value dichotomy, was the classification of homosexuality as a disease entity based on hard scientific facts or was it influenced by values in the form of moral judgement? We can ask further, was the classification based on sound reasoning or was it based on emotive reaction?

In consideration of the cause versus effect dichotomy we could ask whether being anxious or depressed causes the effect of addiction to drugs or does being addicted to drugs cause the effect of being anxious or depressed? In some people the former may be the case, in others the latter. Furthermore, as in the example of homosexuality, we may ask whether or not the state of being addicted should really be considered as a disease. Indeed, according to Schaler (2000), until a little over two hundred years ago (around the time of the Enlightenment), the concept of addiction was unknown. Schaler notes that the change of opinion which led to the disease model of addiction did not originate from scientific research, but emanated partly from the moralistic rhetoric of the 19th century anti-opium and temperance movements.

Positivists advocated that moral evils could be eliminated through scientific endeavour. Certainly, boundaries between the study of natural phenomena and people were not as fixed as they are today and it was not unknown to discuss subjects in terms of the 'moral sciences' (Smith 1998). Thus, as a part of 19th century Victorian positivist progress, many medical conditions were newly classified or re-categorised as disease entities according to new 'scientific' theories.

However, in a move away from the challenges to religious

authority which took place during the Enlightenment, there was now a degree of cross-fertilisation between science and religion. For example, the emerging medical profession sought to control substance use by way of a monopoly over prescribing and therefore discouraged self-medication with opium-based products or alcohol. The anti-opium and temperance movements sought to discourage opium and alcohol use for moral purposes. Therefore, both groups had a vested interest in attenuating drug and alcohol use. It was in such a climate that medical professionals began to study the newly specialised area of addiction and classified it as a disease (Berridge 1999).

Schaler (2000) claims that by following the trend to medicalise social deviancy, it became easier to scare people away from alcohol and drug use as this approach emphasised a moral aspect of disease causation and therefore disease symptoms could be viewed in terms of personal responsibility (Berridge 1999). This hybrid theory suited the anti-opium and temperance movements well because the 'disease' of addiction had been authenticated with a scientific label. In this way, we can see how the science versus culture dichotomy becomes important. We need to consider whether all scientific 'fact' can be seen as objective and free from cultural influence, or whether scientific thought reflects cultural and, indeed, moral values.

Scientific recognition, as noted with the above example of addiction, can provide a degree of authority and authenticity that would be otherwise absent. So, we could consider whether or not contemporary scientific knowledge is universal, reliable, unbiased and factual, and is based on rational thought that is applied to empirical evidence. Also, whether it holds the status of axiomatic self-evident truth as opposed to unsubstantiated belief and can be distinguished from 'traditional' or pre-modern knowledge that was generated by religion, superstition, spiritualism, folklore, magic and idealism (Smith 1998). Indeed, we could ask further, whether our scientific knowledge is the mark of a civilised society or if this status is derived from its role in Western culture in opposition to cultures that were dominated by Western colonial powers during the last four hundred years (Smith 1998)?

With regard to the quantitative versus qualitative dichotomy, we could consider whether or not knowledge accumulated across time from a considerable quantity of empirical observations is superior to knowledge based on an in-depth study which elicits the richness of the lived experiences of the individual. For example, in a quantitative research study we might be trying to determine the existence of a gene associated with or responsible for addiction. We might study the DNA of hundreds, if not thousands, of people deemed to be addicted to something and compare the findings to the DNA of an equal number of people deemed as non-addicted in order to see if a particular gene is present or absent. If we did find such an association, we could then perform statistical analysis on the data that we elicit and calculate the probability of being addicted when we possess or lack a particular gene. However, how might we explain the absence of such a genetic sign in a person who quite clearly displays all the behavioural signs of addiction? In this instance we may need to undertake a qualitative study in order to discover the lived experience of a person and to try and elicit what it was that may have happened during their life, perhaps some traumatic event, to cause them to become addicted. Thus, undertaking research can involve making choices and these examples represent the need for criteria to choose which ones to make. However, we will return to both quantitative and qualitative research methods and the possibility of combining the two in later chapters of this book.

When contemplating the evidence versus belief or opinion dichotomy, we may want to consider exactly what constitutes evidence. For example, what constitutes evidence for the effectiveness of a particular intervention intended to address a health or social problem? How strong might this evidence be? Is it generated through rigorous, objective, unbiased, repeated testing of the intervention? Or is belief in the effectiveness based on unquestioning faith in 'handed down' methods, from experienced expert to novice practitioner, based on opinion, idealism and intuition, which are accepted as being tried and tested because they have supposedly stood the test of time? Furthermore, can we take the good intentions of an intervening health or social care professional as sufficient reason to believe their action will improve a particular situation? Sometimes such an intervention may only serve to worsen the situation. Indeed, there have been many disasters in the fields of medicine, nursing and social work that resulted from faith in the good intentions of the professional.

Summary

In order to provide some grounding for the following chapters of the book, during this first chapter, we have embarked upon a brief historical journey. This was to enable contemplation of some of the significant philosophers and thinkers, who have influenced knowledge construction and modern scientific development and whose concepts still underpin approaches to contemporary research. While we have viewed some of the prime movers involved in the scientific revolution, it should be noted that there were many more who are too numerous to mention within the confines of this book.

Since the 'Scientific Revolution' and the march towards modernism, we have seen how confidence in knowledge based on belief, metaphysics, divinity, superstition, spiritualism, intuition, faith, folklore and theological revelations has been gradually undermined by recognition of the need for empirical knowledge based on evidence generated through experience, reasoning (which may however include a degree of intuition), observation and experiment, namely, objective scientific 'truths', these being tempered by a degree of scepticism. We no longer accept, for example, that the world is flat and if we go too near to the edge we will fall off. Equally, we no longer generally believe that the monarch of a nation represents a godly presence on earth. However, there was a time when asking where the evidence was to support such 'truths' as these, based on divine revelation as they were, could have resulted in the enquirer being put to death for heresy.

Clearly though it would be imprudent to suggest that knowledge based on religious faith, or for that matter, knowledge based on any other type of belief system, has been completely superseded by contemporary scientific knowledge. Furthermore, there remain many uncertainties in the world today, some of which we have seen represented by the dichotomies in the above section. Some of these uncertainties are more amenable to being addressed through research than others and some are more amenable to being addressed by particular types of research. It is this research and the related issues that the remainder of this book will be largely concerned with.

In view of and resulting from some of the issues discussed this chapter, growing concerns about unexplained variations in health and social care practice, cost-effectiveness, appropriate utilisation of resources and the need for service user empowerment, have led to increasing recognition of the need for health and social care practice that is evidence-based. Accordingly, such an evidence base needs to be generated through systematic research. It is this increasing reliance on such evidence that will be explored in more detail in the following chapter.

Chapter 2
Evidence-based practice

Introduction

This chapter examines the concept of evidence-based practice (EBP). It covers the introduction of the concept into health and social care, explores some definitions, including what the term 'evidence' entails, considers some criticisms of the concept of EBP, perceived obstacles to it, some arguments in support of it and a general discussion about the merits of EBP with regard to how it has evolved among today's health and social care professions.

The introduction of EBP into health and social care grew from the concept of evidence-based medicine (EBM), a term which first appeared in the medical literature in a paper by Guyatt *et al.* (1992) which hailed a new way of teaching medicine. Throughout this chapter the terms EBP and EBM are often used in much the same context, although this does not suggest that they are completely interchangeable, despite sharing many conceptual similarities.

According to Guyatt *et al.* (1992) EBM largely refers to the process of making decisions about the provision of health care based on evidence derived from clinical research and this de-emphasises decisions based on intuition and unsystematic clinical experience. Having proclaimed EBM as a 'new paradigm', whereby practitioners would be aware of the limitations of the traditional determinants of decision making and they would learn new skills such as literature searching and critical appraisal of existing research evidence, Guyatt *et al.* (1992) stated that EBM directly deals with the uncertainties of clinical medicine. However, they acknowledged that at the same time, there can be no substitute for the insight-based knowledge gained from years of experience and that when definitive evidence is not available, one must fall back on this 'weaker' evidence (Guyatt *et al.* 1992).

Haynes (2002), one of the co-founders of EBM, states that the concept originated from clinical epidemiologists at McMaster University (Guyatt *et al.*1992). Haynes (2002) noted that applied research methods were originally rooted in clinical epidemiology and that Cochrane in the United Kingdom (UK), Feinstein in the United States of America (USA) and Sackett in Canada, all pioneered and legitimised the use of experimentation in clinical settings (applied research) based on practice-relevant questions, as opposed to in laboratories (basic research). Advocates of EBM propose that experts are more fallible in their recommendations of what works and what does not work than is evidence derived from sound systematic observation, especially so given that in recent decades applied research methods have been developed for use in increasingly complex clinical settings (Haynes 2002).

The fundamental assumption of EBM is that practice based on evidence from applied health care research will provide superior health care compared to that reliant on understanding of research into basic mechanisms (such as the biology of the human body) and clinical experience (Haynes 2002). According to Sackett (1996) such evidence may invalidate previously accepted interventions and tests and replace them with new ones that are more powerful, more accurate, efficacious and safer. However, this assumption is based on the notion that if clinicians are to provide optimal care then they need to know enough about applied research principles to detect published studies that are scientifically valid and ready for application (Haynes 2002).

According to Sackett (1996) it is when asking questions about therapy that we should try to avoid the non-experimental approaches, since these routinely lead to false-positive conclusions about efficacy. Because the randomised controlled trial (RCT), especially the systematic review of several RCTs, is so much more likely to inform us and so much less likely to mislead us, it has become the 'gold standard' for judging whether a treatment does more good than harm (Sackett 1996). This has led to RCTs becoming the hallmark of testing (Haynes 2002). (RCTs will be touched upon later in this chapter and discussed in more detail in Chapter 4 on quantitative research methods.)

Sackett (1996) claimed that doctors practising EBM would identify and apply the most efficacious interventions to maximise the quality and quantity of life for individual patients and this may raise rather than lower the cost of their care. Thus, Sackett (1996) defined EBM as the *conscientious, explicit* and *judicious* use of current best evidence in making decisions about the care of individuals.

- Being conscientious implies having a sense of duty, having the knowledge to justify one's claims to professional expertise, undertaking continuing learning and development, (lifelong learning) and adapting new knowledge to practice with regard to what is effective, ineffective or harmful (Sackett 1996, Newman *et al.* 2005).

- Being explicit means expressing what is meant by consideration of different options, making clear (transparent) on what basis decisions are made and describing what underpins the rationale for practice (Sackett 1996, Newman *et al.* 2005).

- Being judicious means exercising sound, professional judgement (Sackett 1996). This includes recognising that evidence-based judgement should not rest on knowledge of relevant research alone, because despite this often being based on studies that have used large numbers, it may not be appropriate at an individual level (Sackett 1996). Thus, decision making with regard to individuals must also be informed by professional judgement based on intuition, and an intimate knowledge of individual needs and requirements (Sackett 1996, Newman *et al.* 2005).

Noting fears that EBM might be hijacked by purchasers and managers to cut the costs of health care, Sackett (1996) claimed that EBM was not concerned with cost-cutting and this would not only be a misuse of EBM but would suggest a fundamental misunderstanding of financial consequences. However, in a review commissioned by the Health Development Agency into perspectives on EBP, Marks (2002) stated that in addition to any scientific merits, issues of cost containment, quality assurance and the purchaser-provider split in the internal market of the National Health Service (NHS) have influenced the shift towards EBM in the UK.

Research issues in health and social care

According to Elstein (2004), some 25 years ago, the concept of EBM was combined with the psychology-based discipline of decision analysis (DA) which then began to be applied to the field of medical decision-making (MDM). Thus, driven by a combination of interests in the rapid growth of medical technology and treatment options, concerns over inappropriate variations in clinical practice, concerns of cost-effectiveness, increasing patient-empowerment and interest in psychological research into judgement and decision-making, from the early 1980s onwards there was renewed interest in the application of EBM and MDM to health care services in the developed world (Elstein 2004).

Elstein (2004) states that while both EBM and MDM emphasise a quantitative approach to guiding decision making in practice, EBM, with an emphasis on knowledge generation, attracted more interest in the realm of academic medicine. MDM, with an emphasis on how judgement is made, remained the interest of a relatively small scholarly community, particularly those more concerned with psychological research and health policy analysis (Elstein 2004).

Terminology box

Evidence-based practice

- The conscientious, explicit and judicious use of current best evidence in making decisions about the care of individuals

- Having a sense of duty and the knowledge to justify claims to professional expertise, undertaking continuing learning and development and adapting new knowledge to practice with regard to what is effective, ineffective or harmful

- Expressing consideration of different options, making transparent on what basis decisions are made and describing what underpins rationale for practice

- Exercising sound, professional judgement in recognising that evidence-based judgement should not rest on knowledge of relevant research alone, because this may not be appropriate at individual level, which may require professional judgement based on intuition, and an intimate knowledge of individual needs and requirements.

EBP

EBP

Subsequently, the popularity of EBM spread from medicine to other health care professions such as nursing and then into the realm of social care. Thus, the word 'medicine' became replaced with 'practice', giving rise to the more generic term 'EBP'. However, while the actual term may be relatively modern, the general concept of EBP is said to be a revival of an older approach (Elstein 2004, Newman *et al.* 2005). Indeed, according to Sackett (1996), EBM has origins in early 19th century Paris. Thus, it could be argued that it was the 'philosophes', as described in Chapter 1, who in their desire for knowledge based on experience and experiments, as opposed to knowledge based purely on intuition or faith, were the originators of EBM. Given that the philosophes were not only concerned with the practice of medicine, then by implication they can also be seen as the forerunners of EBP.

According to Parahoo (2006) EBP is a reaction to over reliance on experience and intuition and the lack of updated knowledge on the effectiveness of interventions. Thus, EBP is concerned with practical questions about interventions such as: Does it work? How does it work? Are there alternatives? (Parahoo 2006). Parahoo (2006) believes that many practitioners have been unaware of what evidence practice should be based on, or even if any evidence exists at all, and that interventions were often based on the notion that 'it's always been done this way'. Furthermore, variations in practice represent something of a 'lottery' and unnecessary practice, whether benign or harmful, is nonetheless costly (Parahoo 2006). Despite Sackett's (1996) earlier claim, Parahoo (2006) states that due to the general increasing costs of care and particularly the increasing cost and availability of drugs, investment in EBP will bring returns in cost savings.

In their useful book on EBP for Social Workers (SWs) Newman *et al.* (2005) state that all health and social care professionals are now expected to take responsibility for maintaining and improving their knowledge and skills. In a multidisciplinary setting, where EBP is now the rule rather than exception, professionals will all have similar expectations regarding respective strengths and weaknesses of different types of professional knowledge and they need a common language to express this.

Research issues in health and social care

In support of this requirement, a range of UK organisations now collect, produce and disseminate evidence reviews, including the National Institute for Health and Clinical Excellence (NICE) and the Social Care Institute for Excellence (SCIE). NICE is responsible for providing national guidance on the promotion of good health and the prevention and treatment of ill health. NICE (2007) guidance is developed using the expertise of the NHS and developed by a number of independent advisory groups and the wider health care community including: NHS staff, health care professionals, patients and their carers, the public, industry and the academic world. NICE (2007) development processes are underpinned by the key principles of basing recommendations on the best available evidence and involving all stakeholders in a transparent and collaborative manner. NICE (2007) produces guidance in the areas of: public health, health technologies; guidance on the use of new and existing medicines, treatments and procedures within the NHS and clinical practice; guidance on the appropriate treatment and care of people with specific diseases and conditions within the NHS.

SCIE, perhaps best seen as the social care equivalent of NICE, aims to improve the experience of people who use social care services by developing and promoting knowledge about good practice in the sector (SCIE 2007). Using knowledge gathered from a broad range of diverse sources, SCIE (2007) develops resources designed to support those working in social care and to empower service users.

SCIE (2007) works to disseminate knowledge-based good practice guidance and to involve service users, practitioners, providers and policy makers in advancing and promoting good practice in social care. Furthermore, it aims to enhance the skills and professionalism of social care workers through providing reliable, up-to-date, thoroughly-researched transparent, independent guidance and practical tools (SCIE 2007).

Traditionally, social workers have rarely been expected to pay much attention to literature underpinning their profession and their practice (Everitt, 2002). Until recently, social work training has placed little emphasis on teaching practitioners how to formulate a research question relevant to their work, locate information that may answer it, appraise the quality of the information and incorporate the findings into practice (Everitt, 2002). Furthermore, programmes, projects and research into their effectiveness have been based on goals and standards imposed by outsiders with little attempt to match these with local needs and the wishes of service users (Everitt, 2002).

Accordingly, a recent SCIE (2005) report noted that modernisation requires a research infrastructure capable of shifting the basis of social care towards evidence-based policy and practice. Furthermore, this should comprise a research workforce, funding and national strategic framework, but no such infrastructure currently exists to support social care and social work (SCIE 2005). A high premium is now placed on evidence and ensuring that practice is based on evidence rather than on past practice or current patterns of service (SCIE 2005). However, it was noted that in comparison with primary health care, research in social work demonstrates much less progress in achieving the kind of research infrastructure that would support excellence (SCIE 2005). It was noted further that modern services require an integrated approach between the various agencies providing health and social care and this calls for each agency to have a well-developed evidence base for its interventions (SCIE 2005). Put simply, the report claimed that integrated care will be hindered if social care cannot participate with agencies in basing common policies and practices on evidence (SCIE 2005).

Thus, building on Sackett's (1996) earlier definition of EBM, current definitions of EBP differ in that they incorporate the concept of service user involvement. Newman *et al.* (2005) state that professional decision-making depends on the systematic approach to enquiry and knowledge acquisition, drawing on experience, listening to service users, understanding what transparent, relevant, objective research evidence is, why it is important, where to find it, how to appraise it and apply it. However, Newton *et al.* (2005) believe research evidence should not just be for professionals to make decisions, but also to enable service users to become more active in this process. Also, the quality and effectiveness of care provision and interventions should improve when service users are able to influence delivery by complementing personal experiences with access to independent sources of information on effectiveness (Newman *et al.* 2005).

Parahoo (2006) describes the process of EBP as the formulation of a question, the search for relevant research evidence to answer it, the analysis and synthesis of the findings, dissemination and implementation. This should incorporate expertise, evidence and service user views (Parahoo 2006). Parahoo (2006) believes the main objective of EBP is to increase awareness of the effectiveness of decisions and actions of practitioners, policy makers and educators, to use the most effective interventions, thus reducing waste and eliminating unnecessary practices. This will also have the effect of reducing variations in practice and outcomes and will reduce reliance on expert knowledge and increase transparency of decision making (Parahoo 2006).

Evidence

Evidence

While so far there has been much mention of the term 'evidence', we need to specify what type of evidence we are referring to. As suggested above, ideally, evidence should be generated by research. But how do we grade the importance of such evidence? Presented below is a suggested 'hierarchy' of evidence based on the quantitative research methods used to generate different levels of evidence. The actual types of study that are described will be discussed in more detail in the chapter on quantitative research methods.

This hierarchy draws on and has been adapted slightly from other published hierarchies (Petticrew & Roberts 2003, Newman *et al.* 2005, Parahoo 2006, NICE 2007) and thus represents something of a general compilation of hierarchies.

A systematic review is a scientific strategy intended to limit bias in the systematic assembly, critical appraisal and synthesis of all of the relevant studies on a particular topic. A meta-analysis is a type of systematic review that employs statistical methods to combine and summarise the results of several studies (these will be returned to in later chapters).

The studies that make up systematic reviews and meta-analyses are randomised controlled trials (RCTs). The RCT is an experimental study that is usually utilised to test the effectiveness

> **Terminology box**
>
> ## Hierarchy of quantitative methods
>
> - Systematic reviews/Meta-analysis
> - Randomised controlled trials (RCT)
> - Quasi experiments
> - Observational studies: Case control/Cohort
> - Surveys
> - Case series
> - Consensus of expert opinion
> - Reports of clinical experience of respected authorities.

of an intervention or treatment. Participants are randomly allocated (to avoid bias, i.e. to stop a person choosing which group they wanted to be in) to either a control group or treatment (intervention) group. The results for both groups are then statistically analysed and compared to determine if there was a significant difference in outcome between the groups. Analysis of quantitative research data will be discussed in more detail in Chapter 5.

There are other types of study which are not as rigorous as the RCT, for example, if randomisation does not take place. These are generally known as quasi-experiments. Also there are case control studies, cohort studies, single group pre-post studies, non-experimental descriptive studies such as comparative studies, correlation studies, case control studies, observational studies with no intervention such as a survey, and case series. Again, these will be discussed in more detail in Chapter 4.

Returning to the quantitative and qualitative dichotomy, with regard to qualitative research methods, there is no perceived hierarchy of evidence (although some quantitative purists may argue that qualitative methods are at the bottom of the total hierarchy of evidence), but rather several different general types of research method which are presented below. These methods are utilised within different philosophical approaches which will be discussed in more detail in Chapter 6 on qualitative research methods.

> ### Terminology box
>
> ## Qualitative methods
>
> - Interviews
> - Focus groups
> - Case studies
> - Observational studies
> - Discourse analysis.

Criticisms of EBM and EBP

Noting various commentators' stark use of the term 'evidence' while avoiding discussion on what type of evidence they are advocating or rejecting, Petticrew and Roberts (2003) state that while a hierarchy of evidence is a difficult construct to apply in EBM, this is even more so in the appraisal of social or public health interventions. Petticrew and Roberts (2003) claim there is evidence from a number of systematic reviews that contests the view that the evidence hierarchy is fixed, whereby RCTs should always occupy the top end and observational studies should occupy the lower end. Petticrew and Roberts (2003) also claim that methodologically unsound RCTs are not always better than sound observational studies and that the hierarchical order is dependent on, yet often disregards, the research question being asked. Indeed, because different types of research question are best answered by different types of study, the hierarchy may misrepresent the interplay between the question and the type of research which is best suited to answering it and methodological aptness, that is, focusing on the question, is more important than squabbling over the best research method (Petticrew & Roberts 2003). (This will be returned to in Chapter 3 which discusses some different types of research question.)

Marks (2002) claims that the EBP movement employs a scientific discourse derived from the epistemologies of positivism and realism. This, according to Marks (2002), influences the choice of evidence for EBP, whereby what he calls the 'quasi-experiment' of the RCT is highly privileged in the evidence hierarchy and this is the product of historical, political and economic imperatives. Marks (2002) (sounding somewhat Baconian) warns that worshipping idols such as the RCT could lead to errors in judgement and inappropriate practice. Marks (2002) argues that what is considered to be the best evidence in one context may be the worst in another, evidence being the product of a long line of assumptions and choices at the different levels of: epistemology, theory, methodology and methods, each level informing the next, so the evidence that is the final product is conditioned by the choices made at the prior levels.

Furthermore, the evidence hierarchy may be inverted, whereby qualitative methods are at the top (Petticrew & Roberts 2003) – if of course one assumes that qualitative methods are at the bottom to start with. Petticrew and Roberts (2003) believe that the evidence hierarchy also obscures the synergistic relationship between RCTs and qualitative research methods, both types of research being required in social and public health research. Petticrew and Roberts (2003) argue that a combination of qualitative studies, surveys and expert opinion can facilitate understanding the process of implementation of an intervention and what can go wrong, and further, that merely knowing an intervention works is no guarantee that it will be used.

Indeed, Marks (2002) suggests that it is an error to assume that merely informing people about risks is sufficient to facilitate behaviour change. Interventions designed to improve knowledge can do so, but they cannot successfully bring about behaviour change as the behaviour of patient and practitioner does not conform to the rationality principle (Marks 2002). Marks (2002) describes an intention–behaviour gap; the idea that people normally carry out intentions is a myth. Intentions are fulfilled only some of the time, for example, a practitioner fully informed with the best current evidence may intend to change but may never implement that change.

In support of the abovementioned false assumption, Petticrew and Roberts (2003) cite the example of hand washing, which has been known to reduce cross infection for 150 years. Yet health care workers' compliance with this simple yet effective procedure remains poor, indicating that the most simple and cost-effective intervention will fail if not effectively implemented. A more recent example of non-compliance with evidence is that of anti-malarial drugs still being prescribed to patients who had tested negative for the disease (Lubell *et al.* 2008).

Petticrew and Roberts (2003) go on to ask how complete evidence should be before a recommendation can be made for it to inform practice and how much weight should be given to non-experimental data when making decisions about provision of services or policy making? Interestingly, Haynes (2002), one of the original proponents of EBM is now prompted to ask the same question as to when is research 'ready' for application. Haynes (2002) also asks what are 'best' findings, what is valid health care research and how does one apply this anyway? Haynes (2002) claims that the answers to these questions are only partly as good as EBM advocates had hoped for.

Haynes (2002) states that sometimes the results of studies that are methodologically similar may disagree, yet the findings of observational studies may agree with more 'potent' RCTs, thus holes can be picked in the ascendancy of RCTs in the hierarchy, but there is no way of settling this argument without the existence of a universal standard of truth. Ironically, the advocates of EBM and EBP had envisaged that the systematic review and meta-analysis of RCTs would represent this 'gold standard' (Sackett 1996). Haynes (2002) states further that EBM has the tone of a moral imperative, whereby practitioners ought to keep up to date with advances and offer them to patients, yet this could be costly and may prolong life beyond the point of senescence and misery.

Haynes (2002) notes that advocates of EBM now try to ameliorate this problem by declaring that patient values ought to be incorporated into decisions (as was noted earlier in this chapter in more recent definitions of EBP), but without assuring that we actually know how to do this in practice. Illustrative of this last point, Haynes (2002) sees a continuing ethical tension between consequentialist, population-based origins of epidemiology, which advocate providing the greatest good for greatest number, which generates most of the best evidence that advocates of EBP would like practitioners and patients to pay most attention to, versus a deontological, individualistic approach to medicine, that is, doing the greatest good for each individual patient, which is something medical practitioners are sworn to do. (Ethical issues in research will be discussed in Chapter 11.)

Grypdonck (2006) states that qualitative health researchers have to position themselves in a world that is dominated by EBP, as EBP currently sets the tone in health care research. However, Grypdonck (2006) believes the popularity of EBP is not due to the rationality of its tenets and argues that qualitative research plays an important role in providing the understanding necessary to apply findings from quantitative research properly and safely and is important in developing scholarship. Grypdonck (2006) warns that even in the era of EBP, basic studies about the human experience in illness and regarding human behaviour and meaning in general remain of great value and that we need to treat quantitative findings based on self-report with caution.

Like Petticrew and Roberts (2003), Grypdonck (2006) highlights the importance of qualitative research for judging the desirability of outcomes for success, as while RCT findings may be impressive and potent, they may mean nothing if not complemented by other types of knowledge, such as that generated by qualitative research. Grypdonck (2006) postulates that the concept of EBP may be nothing more than an expression of exaggerated belief in progress, and claims that there are no RCTs proving the superiority of EBP and no evidence to prove that opinion should give way to evidence. Likewise, even Haynes (2002) states that so far no convincing evidence exists to support the fundamental assumption that EBM will provide superior health care. There are no studies with patient outcomes as a measure of success showing that patients whose clinicians practice EBM are better off than those treated by clinicians who do not (Haynes 2002).

Furthermore, Grypdonck (2006) points out that while RCTs test at group level they only provide mean average scores which are likely to exclude patients at extreme ends of the spectrum, including very old and very young people, disabled people and other vulnerable people who are not often represented in RCTs. As these various 'marginal' people are not picked up by random sampling, qualitative theory construction can contribute to awareness of the practitioner of the need to contextualise findings, as every patient could be an exception to the rule (Grypdonck 2006). Indeed, Haynes (2002) notes the lack of satisfactory resolution as to how findings from groups can be applied to the individual, as our understanding of what patients want is primitive and circumstances can vary from place to place. Resources, expertise and patients are often quite different and the same research evidence cannot be applied in the same way, if at all (Haynes 2002).

With regard to nursing practice, Closs and Cheater (1999) observed that evidence-based nursing (EBN) was a different enterprise to EBM, as the nursing profession had not yet generated enough evidence to provide the extensive, scientific body of knowledge needed to underpin EBN. Closs and Cheater (1999) believed that a wide range of methods were needed to build the different aspects of the research evidence base for nursing practice. On the question of what constitutes the best evidence to underpin EBN, Closs and Cheater (1999) proposed that it must be in the public arena, it must be consensible (understood) and consensual (agreed).

Closs and Cheater (1999) also argued that what constitutes the best evidence depends on the question being asked, and the quality and appropriateness of relevant research – opinion being used as a last resort. Evidence is crucial but as well as need for information, a more sophisticated approach is needed to implement EBP, including an understanding of the context in which care is provided as well as the obstacles which prevent individuals, teams and organisations from using evidence to inform practice. (Obstacles to EBP will be discussed in a later section of this chapter.)

Parahoo (2006) states that by far the most contentious issue around EBP is: what actually constitutes evidence? Like other critics of EBP and the hierarchy of evidence, Parahoo (2006) notes that the RCT is often sanitised in that participants are carefully selected to control for confounding variables and to recruit a sample who can complete the study. Despite this, the NHS Research and Development agenda has a preference for RCTs, yet this could lead to missing out on observing individual interactions which are complex and may affect treatment. In contrast to those who think that EBP may afford practitioners less autonomy with regard to applying intuition and opinion in decision making, Parahoo (2006) asks the question, if nurses do not embrace RCTs, will they be marginalised?

Parahoo (2006) asks further whether RCTs are always appropriate in disciplines such as nursing, midwifery and allied health professions and whether interventions not evaluated by RCT are to be seen as inferior. Again like other critics, Parahoo (2006) believes that different questions need different research designs and that some nursing knowledge does not fit neatly with the requirements of EBP, so nurses need to draw on a range of research methods other than the RCT.

Parahoo (2006) also notes that as knowledge derived from expert opinion is said to constitute the lowest form of evidence, any practitioner (or indeed anyone at all) armed with the 'best' available evidence can in theory challenge expert authority. In this way, managers or politicians can challenge variations in practice, inefficient, unnecessary practice and have the potential to override experts. For this reason, once again, despite Sackett's (1996) assurances, skeptics see EBP as a form of care rationing. Parahoo (2006) warns that because decisions made by organisations such as NICE are subjective, are based on probabilities and with regard to high costs, what counts as evidence will be contested. In addition, as Youngblut and Brooten (2001) note, the rise of consumerism, information technology and internet access to information now enables patients to gather their own evidence to challenge professional decisions.

Echoing Haynes (2002), in terms of ethics, Parahoo (2006) perceives EBP as being population-based rather than individual-based, thus affording the greatest good for the greatest number, but ignoring individual needs. Indeed, stories of patients who are denied potentially life-saving interventions, based on probabilities of success and relative cost, are frequently reported in the media.

Parahoo (2006) observes that while there is little consensus on what EBN or EBP in nursing means, EBP has revolutionised the way evidence is perceived and its importance in practice and the production, review, appraisal and dissemination of evidence has become a science in itself. Parahoo (2006) believes that EBP will continue to develop, but asks whether it will reduce variations in practice, ineffective practice and save money on a significant scale. He predicts that the future of EBP depends on its own evidence of effectiveness and, like Haynes (2002), thinks that ironically the RCT is unlikely to be the choice of design for generating this evidence.

Marks (2002) warns that given the current political interest in reducing health inequalities, the role of power and ideology in the generation of evidence or 'facts' must be carefully analysed. Furthermore, researchers have the power to distort, overlook, make invisible, exaggerate and draw conclusions based not on factual data, but on assumptions, value judgements and misunderstandings, thus while they may have the potential to extend knowledge, they may also perpetuate ignorance (Marks 2002).

Once again, in agreement with others, Marks (2002) believes that if the choice of method is based on the purpose of the research rather than on epistemological assumptions, then different methods can be combined in order to gain diverse knowledge and complementary insights that can be used to elaborate understandings. Thus, Marks (2002) says we should not ask which method is best, but rather, what can be learned from each perspective?

Marks (2002) claims that currently, we are subjected to the 'mythology' of EBP, this based on a naïve version of positive realism that relies on false epistemological assumptions. For example, the opinion elimination myth is wrong, because opinion and evidence are both needed in decision making (Marks 2002). This again links to the evidence versus opinion/belief dichotomy posited in Chapter 1. Furthermore, Marks (2002) claims that as most decisions are based on out of date evidence, opinions, preferences and routines, 'opinion-based practice' (OBP) may be a more appropriate term, because all beliefs are opinions and we change our opinions much less than evidence indicates – prior opinions influence us more than evidence does.

According to Marks (2002) evidence consists of negotiable, value-laden, contextually dependent items of information and the knowledge base in science and medicine is the result of biases that operate as filters in the context of an establishment with vested interests in preserving existing practices, traditions and myths. For example, the reality derived from systematic reviews is a highly selective and particular one, based on publications in journals, which are reliant on the judgements of editors and peer reviewers who have a predisposition to accept some kinds of evidence and reject others.

Marks (2002) concludes that the adoption of EBP has been slower and less conscientious than its advocates had hoped and that EBP-trained practitioners are unable to carry it out with anything like the skill it was hoped they would. Marks (2002) thinks that the idea that EBP will improve health care and reduce errors is optimistic and may also be risky if the evidence base is incomplete (Marks 2002). Until EBP is shown to be better than OBP, wide scale adoption of the former will be a matter of faith, as the policy to use EBP has no evidence to support it (Marks 2002).

Marks (2002) recommended that it will be necessary to:

- broaden the epistemological approach and evidence base for EBP
- create more inclusive methods for synthesis of evidence
- dispel current assumptions and mythology, replacing these with theory and assumptions that are themselves evidence-based
- employ more sophisticated approaches to the implementation of EBP, that take account of the organisational and psychological barriers to change.

A paradigm shift?

A paradigm shift?

Guyatt *et al.* (1992) proclaimed EBM as a new paradigm. Like Marks (2002), Haynes (2002) observes that most advocates of EBM give little or no thought to constructing a philosophical basis for their activities. In the basic research that underpins traditional medicine, instruments that are objective and bias free are used in discovering basic mechanisms of disease (such as in the example of working with DNA in Chapter 1 [p17]); these mechanisms are then discerned to be a certainty, for example, Newton's law of gravity. Haynes (2002) notes that in contrast, applied research deals with more complex phenomena, which often rely on experimentation and on probabilities to judge the truth rather than expecting certainty. Haynes (2002) ponders as to whether these approaches are mutually exclusive, as would be in a paradigm shift, or as to whether they are complementary ways of knowing, as in a pluralistic version of epistemology. The latter seems more tenable to Haynes (2002).

Closs and Cheater (1999) note resistance to EBP due to what they call 'paradigmatic entrenchment', however, in this context, they suggest that the qualitative versus quantitative debate is increasingly anachronistic and irrelevant. Closs and Cheater (1999) suggest further that EBP does not have to devalue individual nurses' skills, as high quality evidence can comprise the best available toolkit for nurses to use in providing care and how nurses use it in agreeing care with patients and other carers hinges on their experience and expertise.

Sehon and Stanley (2003) observe that while EBM has gained considerable currency over the past decade, critics claim there is no evidence that EBM provides better medical care (as noted by other commentators) and they pose the question as to whether the introduction of EBM represents a paradigm shift. Sehon and Stanley (2003) question further as to whether advocates of the term EBM have a philosophical theory of evidence, according to which everything that has passed for evidence prior to the EBM movement was not evidence at all. However, they suggest that what separates EBM from other approaches is the priority given to certain forms of evidence, and note (as others have done) that the most highly prized form is from RCTs, thus EBM refers essentially to the practice of taking RCTs as the strongly preferred form of medical evidence (Sehon & Stanley 2003).

Citing Thomas Kuhn (1970), Sehon and Stanley (2003) claim that 'normal science' takes place when the scientific community shares a paradigm, that is, an entire constellation of beliefs, values and techniques. They state that Kuhn suggests that history is characterised by mostly normal science, however sometimes a paradigm undergoes a crisis followed by a revolution that overthrows the old paradigm, replacing it with a new one, whereby scientists then respond to a different world (Sehon & Stanley 2003), for example, the shift to the heliocentric model of the solar system described in Chapter 1). However, Sehon and Stanley (2003) suggest that EBM is so intertwined with and complementary to basic science that it would make little sense to see EBM as a paradigm shift away from it and they ask whether the shift away from experience toward favouring RCTs is enough to count as a paradigm shift. They argue that talk of a paradigm shift unduly polarises the debate about the value of EBM, fosters the impression that an entire set of beliefs, values and techniques have been left behind and that the whole world of research and practice is completely different to what it was before EBM was recognised. They suggest that if the claims for EBM are exaggerated this will intensify the natural defensiveness of those who do not feel completely in line with the new regime and that this is not a productive atmosphere in which to hold a debate (Sehon & Stanley 2003). Thus, it is a philosophical and practical mistake to consider EBM as a paradigm shift (Sehon & Stanley 2003).

However, Smith (1998) notes that the meaning of the concept of paradigm is open to question. Indeed, Masterman (1970) identified over 20 different uses of the concept of paradigm by Kuhn. Kuhn (1970) revised his definition of a paradigm to mean a disciplinary matrix, consisting of a strong network of commitments, these being theoretical, instrumental and method-ological. Despite this, there are many and varied uses of the concept of paradigm in the natural and social sciences, it often loosely being used to describe a model, a school of thought, a tradition or a perspective (Smith 1998).

Obstacles to EBP

Obstacles to EBP

There are a number of perceived obstacles or barriers to EBP, which may be viewed separately to the above criticisms, as these are perhaps best described as largely logistical rather than episte-mological. (Marks 2002) describes barriers to the implementation of EBP as follows:

- time constraints
- practitioner stress
- low morale
- poor communication
- resistance to change

- low awareness of evidence
- the absence of computers or training to use them and the internet
- evidence not being considered absolute
- the failure of journals to disseminate information in a practitioner friendly way that motivates them to change practice
- lack of support
- practitioners not sufficiently prepared to evaluate research
- existence of practice routines and hierarchical structures not amenable to change
- practitioner influenced by convictions of training, routines, habits, personal ambitions and the need to conform rather than innovate.

Other commentators echo the above perceived obstacles to EBP. With regard to social care, Newman *et al.* (2005) cite:

- a lack of familiarity with literature
- lack of access to literature and reading time
- lack of critical appraisal skills
- the need to meet performance targets
- staff shortages
- concerns that knowledge accumulated through research of a quantitative nature will serve to attenuate practitioner knowledge that is derived from experience, intuition and insight.

With regard to nursing, the requirement for EBP dictates that nurses are increasingly required to gather evidence themselves. For example, White and Taylor (2002) point out that the United Kingdom Central Council for Nursing, Midwifery and Health Visiting (UKCC) has determined that all first-level nurses should be capable of searching evidence bases, analysing and critiquing research, disseminating research findings and changing practice where necessary. White and Taylor (2002) argue that the UKCC expectations are unrealistic. First, given that medical practitioners have problems with the amount and complexity of published material, the majority of first-level nurses are not going to manage this task without higher levels of training. Second, the process of locating, accessing, critically appraising and then integrating research evidence into practice is prohibitively time-consuming for the average practitioner, often working in units that are under-staffed. Third, by suggesting that research findings should be integrated into practice where necessary, the UKCC model assumes that clinical nurses are autonomous practitioners who are able to supercede the prescribed practices of the organisations within which they are employed (White & Taylor 2002). Similarly, there are barriers to nurses overcoming what can be described as the 'research–practice gap'. These include:

- time constraints
- problems in accessing research findings
- lack of necessary knowledge and search skills to assess such findings
- lack of confidence to incorporate them into practice
- the culture of health care environments.

Closs and Bryar (2001) noted a lack of confidence in nurses' ability to evaluate and implement research, problems in the accessibility of research reports, also the necessary time, facilities and co-operation of doctors and administrators. Barriers also arose through nursing attitudes, in particular, scepticism about the benefits to practice from research (Closs & Bryar 2001). Caine and Kenrick (1997) found that while in principle NHS managers were willing to facilitate EBP, they were doing little in practical terms to foster the necessary environment and resources for research to occur and for the findings to be integrated into practice. The responsibility for EBP was ultimately deferred to carers themselves. Furthermore, some managers may lack advanced academic skills themselves, may perceive research as elitist and may be apprehensive about fostering a highly skilled and analytical nursing workforce (Caine & Kenrick 1997).

With regard to doctors, Haynes (2002) recognised that they too often have limited time and understanding of research methods. Haynes (2002) predicted that it would be difficult for doctors to read at least 19 papers a day in order to keep up with latest research findings, of which very few would be relevant to changing specific practice anyway. However, resources have been created to help practitioners meet these challenges (Haynes 2002).

Arguments in support of EBP

**In support
of EBP**

Despite the abovementioned criticisms and obstacles, there are some positive aspects in support of EBP. It should be remembered that Guyatt *et al.* (1992) acknowledged that there can be no substitute for the insight-based knowledge gained from years of experience. Furthermore, in his paper, on what EBM is, and what it is not, Sackett (1996) emphasised that EBM (this applies equally to EBP) means integrating individual expertise with the best available external evidence from systematic research. Individual expertise means the proficiency and judgement that individual practitioners acquire through experience and practice (Sackett 1996). Increased expertise is reflected in many ways, but especially in more effective and efficient diagnosis and in the more thoughtful identification and compassionate use of individual clients' predicaments, rights, and preferences in making decisions about their care (Sackett 1996).

Thus, decision making with regard to individuals must also be informed by professional judgement based on intuition, and an intimate knowledge of individual needs and requirements (Sackett 1996). As was noted in Chapter 1, this last point serves to remind us that while knowledge based on evidence may be generated through experience and reasoning, this may also include intuition. This point is important, because it is often overlooked by those who criticise EBP, in that de-emphasising intuition may be perceived by those critics as disregarding it completely. This is particularly so in social care where EBP has been associated with the devaluing of context, experience, intuition, insight and the complexity of human interactions (Newman *et al.* 2005).

Sackett (1996) had warned that neither individual expertise or the best available external evidence alone is enough. Without expertise, the risk to practice is that it becomes tyrannised by evidence, for even excellent external evidence may be inapplicable to or inappropriate for an individual client. Conversely, without current best evidence, the risk to practice is that it may become rapidly out of date, to the detriment of clients (Sackett 1996).

As noted earlier in this chapter, basing current practice on past practice (SCIE 2005) and on the way things have always been done (Parahoo 2006) is no longer considered appropriate. To illustrate Sackett's (1996) warning and to emphasise the value of robust evidence for an intervention, it may be helpful to return again to the evidence versus belief dichotomy proposed in Chapter 1. We considered the appropriateness of belief in the effectiveness of a particular intervention, based on unquestioning faith in 'handed down' methods, from expert to novice, which, in the absence of any research-based evidence, are accepted as being tried and tested because they have supposedly stood the test of time and therefore do not need to be replaced.

While it was suggested in Chapter 1 that the Renaissance marked significant reconnection of Western European thinking with the philosophies and teachings of the ancient Greeks, with regard to some aspects, there was never a complete disconnection. An example can be seen in the ancient 'humoral theory' on which the treatment of hysteria was based, leading to interventions for which there was no robust scientific evidence, yet which persisted for centuries.

According to the humoral theory there are four 'humours' in the human body: black bile, yellow bile, phlegm and blood. Depending on whether or not these humours were in balance, people were respectively described as being of a melancholic, phlegmatic, choleric or sanguine type of personality. Imbalances were corrected by treatment that included the application of agents that induced blistering, sweating, vomiting, purging of the bowels, hot and cold compresses, poultices, leeches and blood letting – draining off various amounts of blood from certain body parts (Open University 1991, Rawcliffe 1995). The fact that some recipients of this treatment could be literally bled to death was seen as an acceptable side-effect (Rawcliffe 1995).

The word 'hysteria' is derived from the Greek word for the uterus (womb), 'hustera' (Open University 1991). Thus, based on the belief that one of the causes of hysteria was undischarged menstrual blood from the uterus, the first line of treatment was often blood-letting. Another cause of hysteria was believed to be that the uterus, not being regularly impregnated with male sperm became restless and too dry, thus becoming lighter and migrating upwards in the afflicted woman's body (Open University 1991, Rawcliffe 1995). It was believed that if this 'condition' was left untreated, the uterus would emit noxious fumes which would rise up further to affect the brain (Rawcliffe 1995). Interventions for this included introducing fetid smells through the mouth to repel the uterus downwards, or fragrant smells through the vagina to lure the uterus back to the correct place (Open University 1991, Rawcliffe 1995). Despite the lack of evidence for the 'migratory uterus', the noxious fumes affecting the brain or the efficacy of the interventions for these supposed conditions, these and many other aspects of humoral theory that were supported by 'expert opinion' have stood the 'test of time'. Indeed, the validity of this theory was largely unquestioned and unchallenged for some 2000 years. Even now, in testament to humoral theory, people are still referred to as being phlegmatic or melancholic.

While humoral theory-based treatment for hysteria is no longer prescribed, the concept of the non-impregnated womb being a troublesome organ, responsible for disorders that are not entirely physical in nature, has persisted. This is reflected in the long-running debate over perceived unnecessary hysterectomy (surgical removal of the womb). This debate began in earnest in 1946 when an American gynaecologist published a paper titled 'Hysterectomy: Therapeutic Necessity or Surgical Racket?' (Miller 1946). Miller (1946) reviewed the medical records of all women admitted to ten American hospitals in the first four months of 1945, who had undergone hysterectomy. To his amazement, Miller (1946) found that in 31% of cases, pathological examination of the uterus found no evidence of disease. Furthermore, 10% of women had originally sought medical intervention for conditions such as fatigue, irritability, nervousness and headache. Miller (1946) declared that if this trend could be repeated by future studies, this would represent a tragedy which was painful and far reaching in its implications. Accordingly, it could be argued that as further testament to humoral theory, this is in some way reminiscent of the concept of the non-impregnated, troublesome, restless womb having an adverse effect on women's brains.

Indeed, some two decades later, another American gynaecologist stated that the uterus has but one function, that being reproduction and that after the last intended pregnancy the uterus becomes a useless, bleeding, symptom-producing organ which is potentially cancerous and therefore should be removed (Wright 1969). Thus, despite Miller's (1946) concerns, in recent times, hysterectomy has become one of the most common forms of surgery in the Western world (Open University 1991). The justification for this trend is still questionable because this is not uniform across countries, as was demonstrated by a study which found that in Scandinavia, where menorrhagia (painful bleeding from the womb) is effectively managed by drug treatment, the hysterectomy rate is less than half that of the United Kingdom (UK) (Bonnar & Sheppard 1996). Furthermore, treatment is not even uniform within countries. A UK study of 885 records of female patients who were treated for menorrhagia at 11 practices revealed that substantial variations in investigation, prescribing and referrals (resulting in hysterectomy) persist (Grant *et al.* 2000).

However, Grant *et al.* (2000) noted that a RCT had shown that in UK practices which had received an educational intervention of evidence-based guidance, an improvement in medical management through drug treatment and appropriate referral of women with menorrhagia had been demonstrated (Fender *et al.* 1999). Thus, based on this evidence, it would appear that the application of EBP has the capacity to attenuate variations in practice and therefore reduce the likelihood of unnecessary surgery.

There are other long-running debates over unnecessary surgical operations, a prime example being concerns over tonsillectomy rates among children (Gordon & Cameron 2000). In the 1920s the American Child Health Association studied a sample of 1000 11-year-olds in New York City (Millenson 1997). They found that 61% of the children had already had a tonsillectomy and of the remaining 39% who were sent for screening to doctors, 45% of this group were diagnosed to be in need of tonsillectomy. The remainder of this group was sent for screening again and 46% of them were advised to have tonsillectomy. This process was continued until only 65 of the original cohort of 1000 had not been advised to have tonsillectomy.

Debate about the indications for tonsillectomy continued and during the 1950s when half of all children in America had tonsillectomies, there was still no firm evidence base to indicate the effectiveness of the procedure. Indeed, by the 1970s between 50% and 70% of tonsillectomies performed on children in

America were deemed unnecessary and the rate of operations began to decline (Gordon & Cameron 2000). However, despite this realisation, once again, as with hysterectomy, there is still variation between countries with regard to selection of children for tonsillectomy (van den Akker *et al.* 2004). Furthermore, there is wide variation in tonsillectomy rates across the UK, reflecting differing criteria for diagnosis of tonsillitis and indications for performing tonsillectomy, it being claimed there is a paucity of high quality evidence to support surgical intervention (van den Akker *et al.* 2004). Thus, once again, a high priority is placed upon expert opinion.

Discussion

Having considered the origins and some of the perceived weaknesses and strengths of EBP, it could be surmised that it looks increasingly as though the debate on EBP is turning full circle. Haynes (2002), one of the self-acknowledged founders of the movement, now asks whether or not EBP is a waste of time and if we lack adequate understanding of practical methods of changing practitioner and patient actions. Also, he asks whether EBP really is a new paradigm and whether applied research is more valid than basic research into patho-physiological mechanisms and unsystematic observation (Haynes 2002).

Haynes (2002) acknowledges that today, methodologies from other disciplines are being added to EBP, such as non-experimental and qualitative methods adopted from social sciences. Haynes (2002) also believes that while basic science alone does not provide valid and practical guidance to practice, basic research and applied research are the ends of a spectrum of health research, running from laboratory bench to the bedside, these ends being complementary, as opposed to competing 'best' ways of knowing. Indeed, Haynes (2002) recognises that some of the best applied research is based on basic science findings. Haynes (2002) suggests that confusion between the objectives of science and those of health care practice may have led to much of the criticism and misunderstanding of EBP.

Echoing Marks (2002), Haynes (2002) now advocates a more

pragmatic approach to EBP. Haynes (2002) claims that while EBP was never intended to be a 'cookbook' approach whereby people are treated according to a formula, this was not initially clearly emphasised. However, Sackett (1996) did state that evidence-based medicine is not 'cookbook' medicine, because it requires a bottom-up approach that integrates the best external evidence with individual clinical expertise and patient-choice, therefore it cannot result in slavish, cookbook approaches to individual patient care. However, this may have fallen on deaf ears. Perhaps more significantly, Haynes (2002) points out that it was not initially clearly emphasised how research evidence, clinical circumstances and patients wishes can be combined to derive an optimal decision.

Haynes (2002) states that while clinicians often collect evidence of patients' wishes and circumstances, evidence has been narrowly defined as having to be in the form of systematic observations (reviews) of certain types of research. Thus, according to Haynes (2002) the very term 'evidence' has been an impediment to getting across the message that health care research is now producing important results, that if applied can benefit patients more than treatments that clinicians are experienced in recommending.

With regard to social care, Newman *et al.* (2005) advocate that service users have the right to expect that professionals have the necessary authority to do their job and that sound professional judgement and decision making needs to be informed by research-based evidence as well as experience gained from practice. Assessment and intervention need to be undertaken drawing on knowledge which combines use of the most valid and reliable tools, familiarity and understanding of such tools, appreciation of the particular circumstances of the service user, for example, different culture, the context of the activity and familiarity with the research that underpins such activity and the capacity for reflective and critical thinking (Newman *et al.* 2005). As noted in Chapter 1, practitioners should not be able to claim professional authority based on good intentions alone, as there is the danger of assuming that wherever there is a health or social care need, that the intervention of a professional will automatically improve the situation (Newman *et al.* 2005). There is a need for an approach that involves a robust yet fair evidence-based scrutiny of claims to professional authority (Newman *et al.* 2005).

EBP cannot provide universal, conclusive answers to practice problems and cannot diminish professional experience or service user perspectives (Newman *et al.* 2005). However, it can enable comparison of claims of competing intervention approaches and combine knowledge with views of service user and professional experience to make best possible decisions (Newman *et al.* 2005). Challenging authoritarian views and how professionals justify their status, brings further challenges but has potential to legitimise health and social care interventions (Newman *et al.* 2005). However, despite best evidence, professional judgement is still required in order to decide whether or not to utilise such evidence (Newman *et al.* 2005). Newman *et al.* (2005) believe that to investigate the association between outcome and intervention, the research question can often be approached in different ways and that all have strengths and weaknesses, in fact some may not even answer the question. Some evidence is stronger than others, but it should be acknowledged that sometimes a judgement is required as to what is strong or weak (Newman *et al.* 2005).

The SCIE (2005) report into EBP notes that in social care, effective intervention in the front line requires research that derives directly from practice concerns and offers solutions designed and tested to be feasible in practice. For example, while it is critical to understand the causes of poor parenting or old-age abuse, basic research of this kind does not create an evidence base about effective intervention (SCIE 2005). As a practice research discipline, social work research (at its best) can do this and the rigour and relevance of social work research should be seen as informing the field of social care as a whole and service users should be involved in determining what research processes and outcomes matter (SCIE 2005). The experiences, wishes and needs of service users are central to the production of useful and relevant knowledge in social care (SCIE 2005).

The SCIE (2005) report recommends that progressive approaches within social work research should seek a collabora-tive partnership with the community of practitioners to identify their priorities and how knowledge can be integrated with existing practice, or can effectively challenge it, and to test the day-to-day feasibility of interventions. The current disparity between health care and social care research reduces the effectiveness of social care in delivering welfare and reducing inequalities stemming from social factors (SCIE 2005).

SCIE (2005) recognises that research is a key component of best practice and that there is a need to encourage a higher number of practitioners to be engaged in research if the knowledge base of social care is to be improved. Furthermore, closeness to practice is a major strength not being fully utilised, as knowledge production needs research evidence that can be used in practice, and this begins with practice-relevant questions and ends with relevant material that can be applied (SCIE 2005).

SCIE (2005) also recognises that a wide range of disciplines should play a role in generating evidence for social care, however, social care requires evidence from social work as the primary discipline rooted in social care practice. This should not be limited to the activities of social workers as a wide range of social care activities deserve study (SCIE 2005). Modern forms of knowledge production are increasingly recognised as methodologically interdisciplinary and social work and social care create their own knowledge; the relevance of knowledge should be the hallmark and not a particular approach to research methodology (SCIE 2005).

An example of the above description of modern forms of knowledge generation is Grypdonck's (2006) emphasis that while quantitative research evidence can prove something has an effect, qualitative research evidence can provide an understanding of how or why this may be. Indeed, qualitative research is the most important approach in bringing the perspective of the person to the fore, with regard to appropriateness of an intervention, particularly with regard to what it is like to live and cope with chronic illness (Grypdonck 2006). Furthermore, as previously noted, interpretation of a particular situation is not always easy with quantitative research; there is a need to create and understanding meanings (Grypdonck 2006).

According to Grypdonck (2006) clinical expertise is the integration of scientific findings, reflected experience, observations, and knowledge, synthesised across time and continually adapted to reflect new information and experiences, a process with which qualitative research can help. Grypdonck (2006) believes that EBP is here to stay, but that qualitative researchers must not let their research become undermined and be continually aware of the 'gate-keeping', or what Marks (2002) would call filtering, that quantitative researchers undertake through facilitating publication of quantitative findings in high impact journals.

Interestingly, on reflection, the above commentaries on social care research and qualitative research in this section are not so far out of synchronisation with the founders of EBP. For example, Sackett (1996) stated that evidence-based medicine is not restricted to RCTs and meta-analyses, as it involves tracking down the best external evidence with which to answer clinical questions. Sackett (1996) explains that to find out about the accuracy of a diagnostic test, we need to find proper cross-sectional studies of patients clinically suspected of harbouring the relevant disorder, not a randomised trial, and for a question about prognosis, we need proper follow-up studies of patients assembled at a uniform, early point in the clinical course of their disease.

Sackett (1996) emphasises that external clinical evidence can inform, but can never replace, individual clinical expertise, and it is this expertise that decides whether the external evidence applies to the individual patient at all and, if so, how it should be integrated into a clinical decision. Similarly, any external guideline must be integrated with individual clinical expertise in deciding whether and how it matches the patient's clinical state, predicament, and preferences, and thus whether it should be applied (Sackett 1996). According to Sackett (1996), clinicians who fear top-down cook-books will find the advocates of evidence-based medicine joining them at the barricades. One point remains though, regardless of Sackett's (1996) claim that EBM would not be cost-cutting medicine, fears that EBP in general would be hijacked by purchasers and managers to cut the costs of health care seem to have been borne out. So we may ask: does this constitute a misuse of evidence-based medicine and a fundamental misunderstanding of EBP's financial consequences?

Haynes (2002) believes that EBP has now evolved into a less pretentious and more practical approach and must continue to evolve and agree on what constitutes best evidence, and facilitate appropriate, efficient communication between patients, practitioners and policy-makers. Also, moral issues, including distributive justice and individual autonomy need to be addressed (Haynes 2002). Haynes (2002) concludes that given the high investment in research and the high expectations of society in reducing the burden of ill health, attention to these matters should have high priority.

Marks (2002) states that, given that public health, health promotion and health education (and nursing and social work) are applied disciplines that are concerned with psychological mediating processes as much as physical outcomes, it is necessary to adopt an epistemological framework such as critical realism or pragmatism that can integrate both evidence on processes, subjective experience and socio-cultural meanings and evidence on the effects of interventions. Therefore it will be necessary to broaden the epistemological approach and evidence base, create more inclusive methods for synthesis of evidence, dispel current mythology and replace it with theories and assumptions that are themselves evidence-based and employ more sophisticated approaches to implementation that take account of barriers to change.

Marks (2002) predicts that if health care (this applies equally to social care) is to become truly evidence-based then the current positivist approach will require radical change. Within the spectrum of extreme positivism and empiricism at one end and extreme relativism and idealism at the other, intermediate positions allow for the realist view that there is an objective physical reality independent of prior knowledge and also the constructionist view that human interpretation and subjective meanings configure multiple social worlds and a diversity of truths.

Summary

Despite various shortcomings, criticisms and barriers, given the resources that have been put into organisational networks such as NICE and more recently SCIE and despite Sackett's (1996) hopes that EBP would not result in cost cutting, as Closs and Cheater (1999) note, EBP will be necessary if we are to provide clinically effective and cost-effective care to an increasing population.

Indeed, the economics of health and social care resources is a major issue in contemporary society and for this reason alone it is likely that despite the various perceived barriers (Caine & Kenrick 1997, Closs & Bryar 2001, Marks 2002, White & Taylor 2002), questions over the evidence for effectiveness of EBP (Grypdonck 2006, Haynes 2002, Marks 2002, Sehon & Stanley 2003, Parahoo 2006) and suggestions that it has an ideological status (Marks 2002), EBP will be here to stay. Furthermore, there is an ongoing requirement for claims based on anecdote or personal experience to be tested and independently verified.

However, as EBP spreads and diffuses through the various professions and disciplines, it is likely that it will necessarily evolve accordingly into the appropriate form or forms relevant to each particular context, such as the particular evidence required in the context of the type of research question being asked (Sackett 1996, Marks 2002, Closs & Cheater 1999, Haynes 2002, Parahoo 2006). While addressing uncertainty, the antithesis of knowledge, is a basic principle of scientific enquiry, it should be borne in mind that knowledge acquisition is not always straightforward – indeed we may need to modify our views and beliefs when new information emerges. Therefore the following chapter on development of research questions, the first step in generating research evidence, provides further discussion on knowledge and its acquisition.

Chapter 3
Developing a research question

Introduction

As Parahoo (2006) quite correctly points out, the formulation of a research question is clearly fundamental to the research process. Accordingly, this chapter provides a discussion and advice on developing a research question. However, it should be noted that there is no easy formula for doing so, as usually each question is unique, in that it is relevant to the particular problem, issue or interest to be addressed. There are some general requirements though. Basically, a good research question should be clearly stated, it should be unambiguous and it should comprise a concise statement of purpose about what you want to achieve and are trying to find out. Furthermore, the question should be specific, feasible, answerable, justifiable and ideally, as noted in the previous chapter, have the potential to generate findings that will improve health and social care practice.

It should be noted that the research problem, issue or interest to be addressed is often broad, multi-faceted, can be complex and it is not always feasible or even possible to address every aspect through a single research question. More experienced researchers often find that they need to develop a study design which incorporates a number of aims and objectives, represented by several research questions. For the novice researcher though it is usually advisable not to get side-tracked or get pulled in too many different directions and to remain focused on one particular question, albeit one that is often developed and refined to the point whereby it may differ slightly from the original question. Robson (2002) observes that while there is no foolproof, automatic way of undertaking this process, the envisaged sequence usually entails moving from a general, broad research focus to a small number of relatively specific, intuitively reasonable questions, then selecting one of them and refining it further.

In Chapters 1 and 2 you were introduced to the dichotomy between the quantitative and qualitative research approaches and the suggestion that the research approach to be adopted and the perceived quality of the study findings is to some extent dependent on the context and the research question to be answered (Sackett 1996, Closs & Cheater 1999, Haynes 2002, Marks 2002, Grypdonck 2006, Parahoo 2006). However, if the approach to take is not immediately apparent, undertaking a review of literature relating to the problem, issue or interest and examining how others have approached similar, yet not identical challenges, can often be helpful in allowing one to focus on the relevant approach to take in answering the research question. This in turn could be influential in determining a rethink with regard to the nature of the question. However, it is advisable to avoid the temptation of tailoring the research question to fit with a particular approach, although in practice this can happen. For example if the researcher has particular expertise in quantitative approaches and yet is confronted with a question perhaps best suited to a qualitative approach, it may be logical to alter the question to the point where it is best answered by a quantitative design, and vice versa. Having said that, there are many research questions that can be answered equally well by either approach or indeed, answered using a study design whereby both approaches are combined, as objectivity and subjectivity both elicit useful and interesting information. (This will be discussed in more detail in Chapter 8.)

Levels of research question

Levels of research question

Research questions may provide answers that can: describe, explain, identify, qualify, substantiate or even predict something. Accordingly, various taxonomies have been developed for proposed classification of different levels of research question. For example, Brink and Wood (1994) suggest the following levels:

- Level I – Fact finding, exploratory, descriptive, for example, what do we know about certain people's attitudes to something or, what is the prevalence of a particular condition?

- Level II – Concerned with establishing a relationship, for example, what is the relationship between a particular condition and a certain group?
- Level III – Explores why a relationship exists, for example, why does a particular group behave in a certain way?

Robson (2002) proposes a similar order of levels of research question:

- Exploratory – To be applied in little understood situations, to provide new insights and to generate ideas and hypotheses (hypotheses will be returned to in a later section of this chapter)
- Descriptive – To enable an accurate profile of persons, events or situations
- Explanatory – To enable explanation of causal relationships, to explain various patterns.

These levels are not necessarily hierarchical with regard to order of importance, as a Level I or Exploratory question relating to an under researched area may be as important as a Level III or Explanatory question relating to a heavily researched area. Clearly, then the approach to be taken in answering a research question can also be influenced by the level that one is operating at. For example, Level I descriptive questions may be best answered using a qualitative research approach (although it may also be feasible to employ a quantitative approach such as a questionnaire survey to determine the prevalence of something), and Level III questions are likely to be best answered with a quantitative, experimental, testing approach.

Terminology

Terminology

Regardless of the level one is operating at, as stated at the beginning of this chapter, it is important to be as clear and as unambiguous as possible. This means the terminology that we use must be clearly defined. Thus, it is important to provide clear, specific definitions of any obscure or uncommon terms or concepts used, or where there is the potential for ambiguity or misinterpretation.

For example, our research question may be a Level I,

descriptive question and ask:

'What is social workers' knowledge of drug addiction among young people?'

In this case we may first wish to define what we mean by social workers. Do we mean all social workers in general or do we mean social workers who work within youth offending teams and/or social workers who are attached to drug and alcohol units? What do we mean by knowledge? Do we mean knowledge of the prevalence of addiction among young people or the effects of specific addictive drugs, or both? How would we measure this knowledge? How could we design a study to examine this issue without appearing to want to test social workers' knowledge and risk putting them off from participating in such a study, lest they feel they were being judged? Could the number of years experience in the field of dealing with young people who are addicted to drugs be an accurate proxy measure of knowledge? Already we can see that a number of uncertainties have arisen from what may on the surface appear to be a relatively straight-forward descriptive enquiry that does not require any complex experimentation. However, things are likely to become even more uncertain when we start thinking about how to define 'addiction', because, despite this being a term commonly used in contemporary society, we can ask: Do we really know what we mean by this term? Does the term mean the same thing to everybody? For example, is it really a disease as some people claim, as was highlighted in Chapter 1, when it was noted that as part of positivist progress, in attempts to medicalise social deviancy, certain conditions were perhaps inappropriately categorised as disease entities (Schaler 2000).

Indeed, the unstable foundation of Victorian hybrid moral/scientific theory, which underlies the concept of addiction and which serves as a useful example of the science versus culture dichotomy, as introduced in Chapter 1, has resulted in failure to reach consensus on the application of correct terminology in the field of studying recreational drug use. This lack of consensus is reflected in the fact that, according to the World Health Organisation (WHO) international classification of diseases, the disease of addiction does not exist (WHO 1992). The WHO only lists a diagnosis for 'dependence syndrome', this term being adopted because it was realised that some individuals could be physically dependent on a drug, yet without being psychologically dependent on it and/or without compulsively using it and vice versa (WHO 1992). Furthermore, the WHO diagnosis of dependence syndrome is perceived as not being absolute, but existing in degrees, with compulsive drug-using behaviour at the extreme end (WHO 1992). However, in practice, the term 'addiction' is commonly used to impose a category, resulting in people being labeled either as being addicted or not addicted, this type of categorisation reducing the possibility of viewing people as being anywhere in between these extremes. Such problems are highlighted in a recently published book on problematic drug use, in which by way of an 'Author's Apologia', Professor Gossop of the National Addiction Centre in London acknowledges that he chooses to offer no definition for the term 'addiction' and goes on to describe the issue as a 'terminological minefield' (Gossop 2000).

Thus, we need to think very carefully when deciding on the wording of our research questions, because as the above example clearly demonstrates, before we realise it, we may find that we have wandered into the proverbial 'terminological minefield'. We should also remember that each professional discipline, whether within or outside the realms of health and social care, is likely to have a particular specialist terminology which holds specific meaning only for those within a given profession. These terms may also represent ideas and assumptions about the way in which the world is organised and the most appropriate methods for studying it (Smith 1998). Consequently, in this way, certain theoretical assumptions, such as for example, the theory that addiction is a disease entity, will be likely to have an influence on the choice, the development and the wording of research questions. Accordingly, the relationship between theory and research questions is now discussed in more detail below.

Research issues in health and social care

Research questions, theories and hypotheses

Research questions, theories and hypotheses

McKenna (1997) identifies three core elements that exist within any practice-based discipline. These are:

- practice (perhaps not surprisingly)
- theory
- research.

McKenna (1997) describes the association between practice, theory and research as a cyclical process, as follows. Practice leads to theory, theory leads to research and research leads back to practice. In this way, building upon the relationship between knowledge and research as highlighted at the beginning of Chapter 1, whereby it was noted that research is used as a way of creating new knowledge, new theory generated from practice leads to new studies, which leads to new knowledge for practice and this new knowledge presents us with new facts which, in turn encourage us to develop further theories to explain these facts. Thus, research needs to be undertaken in the context of theory but with awareness of how it can contribute to the generation of new knowledge and yet further theory. McKenna (1997) advocates that while knowledge is provided by research, understanding of this knowledge is through theory, thus, knowledge is not much use to us without an adequate understanding of theory.

Echoing the advocates of evidence-based practice discussed in the previous chapter, McKenna (1997) states that practice has often been undertaken without being guided by research or even by any particular theory. For example, according to McKenna (1997) much of the research to inform nursing practice has traditionally been descriptive and poorly linked to theory and studies have continued to be undertaken without cognisance of any theoretical alliance. McKenna (1997) argues that research that is isolated and does not lead to the development of or corroboration of theories is limited in usefulness and the end product of such research is poor if it does not inform theoretical explanations of phenomena, prediction of events, situations, or responses, or the prescription of health care interventions.

Robson (2002) notes that while the research question may first be stimulated by theory, it is then necessary to seek a specific context. However, as noted above, there is no automatic way of selecting a research question and the process may be non-linear, involving considerable uncertainty and intuition, and is likely to be driven by a specific problem needing to be solved. However, it is important during the research question development process not to lose sight of concerns for theoretical understanding and thus confer 'real world' value on the proposed research question and subsequent study design (Robson 2002).

Robson (2002) highlights the distinction between research questions that lead to theory verification or theory generation. The former are generally through studies that employ positivist, quantitative methods, of experimental design, starting with a theory, formulating a hypothesis, statistically analysing and testing data and then determining if the theory is refuted or supported. The latter, theory generation, is generally through studies that employ interpretivist, qualitative, descriptive, exploratory methods which focus on careful, in-depth examination of data to find patterns, starting with no theory and seeking to develop and induce theory through undertaking the study. It should be noted though that while it can be generally summarised that quantitative, deductive approaches to research test theory and qualitative, inductive approaches generate theory, it is also possible to use quantitative research for theory generation and qualitative research for theory verification. (Please note that the quantitative/qualitative research approach dichotomy will be returned to and explored further in later chapters.)

Terminology box

Deduction and induction

Students often become confused with the terms 'Deduction' and 'Induction'. For clarification, in contemporary research usage, deduction can be taken to mean the drawing of logical inferences from statements, such as theories or hypotheses. These inferences can then be tested against evidence, experimental or otherwise, to refute or support, though not conclusively prove, the theory or hypothesis. Induction can be taken to mean the process of arriving at general statements or theories based on the process of observation, description and classification.

Research issues in health and social care

Hypotheses

It is important to point out at this stage that a research question is simply a question that you seek to answer through the proposed study and that a hypothesis is something different, something that is tested by the study. Parahoo (2006) defines hypotheses as educated guesses made by researchers. Thus, putting forward a hypothesis is making a tentative statement about a relationship, if any, between two or more variables. According to Parahoo (2006) a hypothesis must include three components: variables, a population and a proposed relationship. (Hypotheses, variables, relationships and populations will all be returned to in Chapter 4 on quantitative research methods.)

Hypotheses are typically presented in two formats:

- the null hypothesis (H0)
- the alternative hypothesis (H1).

If we have a hypothesis that a particular intervention can improve a particular condition, when we design a study to test this hypothesis, we are not designing a study to prove our hypothesis to be correct, that is, to prove that we are right by demonstrating the positive effect of our new intervention. Rather, we are seeking to suggest that we are not wrong. To support this suggestion of not being wrong, we need to be able to reject the null hypothesis, which is, in effect, a competing hypothesis that states that our intervention will not work in the way that we hope for and that any positive effects will be due to chance rather than the properties of the intervention, for example, that the condition would have improved with time anyway. However, if our study findings tell us that we can reject the null hypothesis, this does not mean that our hypothesis (the alternative hypothesis) can be unconditionally accepted, it only means that it is supported, but not proven to be correct beyond question. This is because we can never be 100% sure that the study findings are true because there is always the possibility, however small, that our results are due to chance. Therefore, statistical testing of the significance of our results is used to determine the probability of our results being due to chance. While these issues will be returned to in Chapters 4 and 5 on quantitative research methods and analysis of quantitative data respectively, for the time being it is important to remember that the term 'hypothesis' should not be used interchangeably with the term 'research question', this being a mistake sometimes made by students.

Research and theory

McKenna (1997) provides a helpful categorisation for viewing different ways in which research and theory can be specifically related. He proposes that there are four main ways in which research and theory interact, as follows:

- theory testing research (deduction)
- theory generating research (induction)
- theory evaluating research
- theory framed research.

We have already been introduced to McKenna's first two categories. As noted above, theory testing research employs quantitative studies that seek to collect data or evidence in order to support or refute the theory. These may be randomised controlled trials (RCTs) or quasi-experimental approaches which may also lead to adaptation or revision of a theory, or a new theory altogether. In this case the boundaries may become blurred between theory testing and theory generation and as was noted earlier, it should not be forgotten that quantitative approaches can also be used for theory generation. However, theory generating research, undertaken when little is known about phenomena, usually employs qualitative studies that involve the process of observation, exploration, description, classification and theory generation.

However, as can be seen, McKenna (1997) introduces two new categories. Those of theory evaluating research and theory framed research. Theory evaluating research may perhaps be seen as being similar to theory testing research, however there are some differences. For example, while it may be suggested that some grand theories cannot be truly tested, we can say that the best we can do is to examine the application of a given grand theory in order to evaluate its usefulness (McKenna 1997). This may contribute to establishing the worth of a theory in practice, the rejection of a theory, the adaptation or revision of a theory or, as with theory testing research, the generation of new theories (McKenna 1997).

Theory framed research, as the name suggests, is research whereby a particular theory frames the study, guiding it and providing it with focus. In addition, this may contribute to establishing the worth of the theory as a framework and may lead to its rejection or adaptation, or even the generation of a new theory. So, once again, in common with the other categories, theory framing research may end up as a form of theory generating research. However, McKenna (1997) warns that there are several potential problems with theory framed research. First, it is necessary to determine if the framework is really linked to the study in a natural way and if an alternative framework would be more appropriate. Second, we need to ask whether the theory merely acts as 'window dressing' thereby lending theoretical credibility to the study. Third, the inappropriate selection of a theory may lead to theoretical vision that is impaired, this having the effect of blocking clear understanding of phenomena. Fourth, the theoretical framework may take on an agenda setting role, bringing with it inherent biases. This is primarily because the selection of any theoretical framework is likely to be value-laden (as also noted by Marks (2002) and introduced in Chapter 2), and therefore likely to influence the perceived benefits of the study, the definition and measurement of concepts, the interpretation and significance of the findings and how any generated knowledge will be utilised (McKenna 1997).

Terminology box

Research and theory

- Theory testing research – tests theory deductively in practice
- Theory generating research – generates theory inductively from practice
- Theory evaluating research – evaluates theory in practice
- Theory framed research – theory guides research in practice.

Values

Values

With regard to the suggestion about the possibility of a given theoretical framework being value-laden and the consequent potential for bias, it should be remembered that all researchers are located within a particular social and cultural context that will be influenced by things such as the researcher's ethnicity and gender and that this will undoubtedly impact on how knowledge is produced. Therefore, when developing a research question it is useful to contemplate and reflect upon how much we draw upon our own values and assumptions when we develop concepts, arguments and collect evidence (Smith 1998, Marks 2002). One of the ways to try to avoid this kind of bias has been the positivist approach, in adopting the methods from the natural sciences such as in the study of physics, in an attempt to become detached from the object of study. Despite this, as McKenna (1997) and Marks (2002) point out, the choice of a research question invariably involves the introduction of values. For example, the simple commitment to producing knowledge entails an assumption that knowledge is preferable to ignorance and that the proposed research study will make an improvement; therefore, the researcher's values are always at play, both in developing research and interpreting the findings (McKenna 1997).

Furthermore, thinking back to the fact versus value dichotomy introduced in Chapter 1, with what degree of certainty can we say that science is value free? For example, let's go back to the research question: 'What is social workers' knowledge of drug addiction among young people?'

If we are operating within a theoretical framework based on the disease model of addiction, how certain can we be that addiction really is a disease? Is this a scientific fact? Or is this classification merely based on Victorian moral values? What other evidence is there? Indeed, given the earlier reference to the 'terminological minefield', how certain can we be about our conceptualisation of addiction as even being in existence? There are no easy answers to these and other fundamental questions that we can find ourselves confronted with when we are merely seeking to develop a clearly defined, feasible and answerable research question.

Research issues in health and social care

Summary

In this chapter we have considered the possibility of developing a clear, unambiguous, feasible research question from contemplating a particular problem, issue or interest to be addressed. To this end, we have considered the importance of clearly defining our terminology. We have looked at some suggested different levels of research question and the relationship between practice, research, theory, hypotheses and the generation of knowledge. However, it is apparent that knowledge systems represent complex series of values, assumptions and methodological rules governing what might constitute appropriate knowledge in a given time and place. Therefore, in the pursuit of our research goals we need to be aware that all knowledge is grounded in historical and social circumstances and to remember that cultural or moral values may be translated into 'scientific facts'.

Furthermore, it will be wise of us to remember that the above factors are likely to guide the research question or questions that we decide upon, and to influence the research approach and the methods that we decide to utilise in answering them. Accordingly, the following four chapters of this book are concerned with different research approaches and methods and the analysis of the ensuing different types of data.

Chapter 4
Quantitative research methods

Introduction

In the first chapter we began to contemplate the quantitative versus qualitative dichotomy and this was expanded upon in Chapters 2 and 3. In Chapter 2 we examined parts of the debate as to whether or not there was a hierarchical distinction between quantitative research and qualitative research, that is, with evidence that is derived from quantitative research perceived as being superior to evidence that is derived from qualitative research. In Chapter 3 we discussed the relevant research approach to take in answering a given research question, whether it may be qualitative or quantitative or a combination of both.

In this chapter we will consider some quantitative research designs including questionnaire surveys, various experiments such as the randomised controlled trial and some other types of study. It should be noted that this chapter will not detail all types of quantitative research, just some of the main, commonly used types. We will also look at some general sampling methods.

Bryman (2004) notes that the characteristics of quantitative research represent a distinct strategy in collecting and analysing data. Although their dominance has declined since the 1970s, quantitative research data still exert a powerful influence on society. Indeed, these types of data can be useful in providing contemporary society with a great deal of knowledge about itself in general, and many types of health and social care organisations use quantitative research data to help inform their actions and decisions. Quantitative research in the social sciences is very similar, if not the same as in the natural sciences and researchers working in the realm of health and social care draw on both types of science. For example, we might conduct a survey to determine what improvements service users and other stakeholders think could be made to certain services provided by a social services unit, as in the social sciences, or we might conduct an experiment to test the biological effect of a substance (for example a new drug) on the human body, as in the natural sciences. Conversely, we might conduct a survey into hospital patients' preferences with regard to particular treatment choices or we might conduct an experiment to determine whether an innovative social services mentoring programme can keep repeat young offenders out of prison.

Terminology box

Quantitative research approach

- Draws on philosophies of empiricism and positivism
- Seeks to establish scientific knowledge through objective, systematic observation
- Can be used to establish causal relationships so that predictions can be made
- May be regarded as synonymous with the traditional scientific method
- Also associated with social sciences
- One reality, the same (or similar) for everyone
- The researcher is neutral, research is value-free and objective
- The setting is often controlled
- The study design is specified before the study starts
- Validity and reliability are important
- Theory is often tested.

However, regardless of the setting in which they are conducted, both survey and experimental research rely largely on quantitative, essentially numerical evidence, based on a belief in the ability to measure and quantify in some way both natural phenomena and social phenomena. The quantitative research approach (or tradition) is associated with a philosophical paradigm with roots in both empiricism and positivism and quantitative studies are usually influenced by and designed to reflect positivist goals (Yates 1998, Parahoo 2006). Thus, quantitative research is informed by a particular ontological and episte-mological position, which reflects a good deal more than just the mere presence of numbers (Bryman 2004).

Positivism

Positivism

The concept of positivism was introduced in Chapter 1. Despite the demise of Auguste Comte, positivism can be seen as a broad movement of thought which marked the second half of the nineteenth century. As noted in Chapter 1, positivism placed emphasis on reason and logic and was deemed to be 'positive' because it offered an objective and true account of nature and society whereby humans would be able to understand the scientific laws which govern the world (Smith 1998). Positivists believed that all phenomena could be explained in the same way, through the scientific method and that only data which are directly experienced are relevant to science. Thus, facts, which could be empirically verified, could be separated from values and only these facts can be regarded as scientific (Smith 1998). Positivists have preference for empirical data, believing that law-like regularities could be generated from quantitative evidence. Further, it is assumed that human behaviour obeys scientific laws and if these scientific laws could be discovered, that is, be generated from general statements based on empirical regularities, based on that which can be observed, measured, replicated and quantified, then social and moral evils and disease could be eliminated (Smith 1998).

Terminology box

Positivism
- Preference for empirical data that can be observed/measured
- Can be viewed as branch of empiricism
- Events explained by rigorous scientific observation
- Assumes a body of independent, objective knowledge which is able to explain, control and predict phenomena under study
- Laws/regularities can be generated from quantitative evidence.

However, as the positivist ethos became increasingly criticised it was subject to a number of challenges and modifications (Smith 1998). The Concept of 'Logical Positivism' held sway for a brief period (see terminology check box and the section below on hypotheses). However, while few researchers would now call themselves pure positivists, as they recognise that not all phenomena are reducible or amenable to objective study, they might call themselves post-positivists (see terminology check box and the section below on hypotheses). Despite this, the influence of positivism remains, although it is now seen as appropriate convention to seek to test hypotheses in order to falsify them as opposed to attempting to verify them to be correct. This will be returned to later in this chapter. It was noted in Chapter 1 that positivism was influenced by the empiricist belief in the requirement for observations and experiments to generate evidence and that the positivist approach represented a further challenge to knowledge based on theological, supernatural and metaphysical explanations of the world.

Terminology box

Logical positivism
- According to logical positivists, there are two sources of knowledge – derived from: logical reasoning and empirical experience
- An example of logical knowledge is that which is derived from mathematics, which is reducible to formal logic
- Need for scientific testing and verification of hypotheses.

Again, as noted in Chapter 1, a number of assumptions are associated with positivism. Positivists advocated that the methods of studying the natural sciences such as physics could be transferred to the social sciences, and that if something cannot be experienced by our physical senses it is metaphysical and therefore cannot be said to exist. Therefore, concepts that cannot be experienced are meaningless. Furthermore, in Baconian fashion, objects of scientific study should be broken down into their smallest constituent parts and examined, this now being known as 'reductionism'. There was also an assumption that words and terms have fixed and universal meanings, for example that the term 'health and social care' has the same meaning to everybody (Smith 1998). However, as was discussed in the previous chapter, this type of assumption is likely to be erroneous.

Terminology box

Post-positivism

- Principle of verification replaced by falsification, i.e. theories/hypotheses should be tested to see if they can be falsified, not verified
- There is a place for intuition and imagination in science
- Recognition of complex nature of world
- Recognition that while some phenomena are reducible for study, others are not.

The general quantitative process

The general quantitative process

In assuming that human phenomena are amenable to objective study and measurement, the social scientific process mirrors the natural scientific method. As noted in the previous chapter, this begins by stating in advance the research question or hypothesis and then operationalising the concepts and terminology. Then the appropriate methods for answering the question or testing the hypothesis and analysing data need to be selected. Findings are then presented, usually in numerical, statistical form. The use of statistics is designed to separate out any effects which may have occurred by chance, this being a form of control or 'closure'. Other forms of closure may be:

- experiments undertaken in closed systems – such as a laboratory
- the ways of selecting the sample to be studied
- fixed questions in a survey to control or remove what is perceived as the undue influence of external factors.

Quantitative research usually starts with a theory, which in this context can be described as a broadly deductive approach, whereby a hypothesis is deduced from a theory, the hypothesis then being tested (Bryman 2004). However, Bryman notes that a great deal of quantitative research does not entail a hypothesis (a hypothesis being more likely in experimental research; this will be returned to later in this chapter), and is often based on a theory acting loosely as a set of concerns or a research question, in relation to which data are collected. However, as previously noted, it is possible to undertake a quantitative study which reveals new evidence that leads to the induction of a theory (McKenna 1997).

Operationalisation then takes place, whereby a concept is defined and measured. Research sites (the setting) and participants (the sample) are then selected, participants are assigned into control or intervention groups (if an experimental study), tools or instruments are administered and information is transformed into data to be quantified and analysed and tested for relationships, to determine if the hypothesis or theory is supported. Following this, ways of presenting the results to others are developed – the researcher must 'interpret' the results of data analysis into findings (Bryman 2004). Thus, quantitative research has evolved as a linear series of steps usually moving from theory, to objective measurement and analysis, to conclusion. This process can be described not only as deductive (although possibly inductive), but as reductionist and deterministic, yielding findings that are expected to be replicable and generalisable (Bryman 2004). Throughout this chapter, the above steps will be discussed in more detail.

Measurement

Measurement

As noted above, quantitative research is largely concerned with the objective measurement and quantification of phenomena. Bryman (2004) sets out three main reasons for measuring: to have a consistent device or 'yardstick', to be able to estimate the degree of relationships between concepts and to be able to delineate fine differences. Noting the central position of measurement in the scientific method, Parahoo (2006) describes this as the systematic process of assigning numbers to persons, objects or events which represent the amount and type of specific attributes to be studied in order to achieve objective, reliable, valid, scientific status for our findings. Bryman (2004) describes these attributes as 'concepts' which can be seen as the building blocks of theory, that is, categories for the organisation of ideas and observations. Bryman (2004) highlights the importance of defining or 'operationalising' our concepts and developing direct measures, or indicators of them. Examples of direct measures are: distance, age, income and number of years spent working.

Bryman (2004) defines an indicator as a way of tapping a concept for which there is no direct measure. For example, intelligence quotient (IQ) is an indicator of the level of a person's intelligence but it is not a direct measure. Similarly, Parahoo (2006) notes the difference between concepts amenable to objective measurement, such as time, height and weight and concepts not amenable to complete objective measurement, such as attitude, satisfaction, tiredness, pain, emotion and belief. Scales are often developed and constructed in order to capture and subsequently measure these concepts, which can lead to a degree of error as they are essentially proxy, value-laden measures, in the same way as our research question can be value-laden (see Chapter 3). Thus, purely objective measures can be considered as more reliable than indicators or proxy measures, particularly those indicators based on self-report. Whether the latter will be accepted as appropriate evidence may depend to some degree on what other evidence is available – in legal contexts, where for example, if DNA material or video tape footage is lacking, evidence appropriate for the circumstances, such as eye-witness testimony, is resorted to. However, whereas in law, practitioners may have the luxury of stating that a particular case cannot progress due to insufficient evidence, in health and social care, this is not usually possible as practitioners are required to intervene, treat or act utilising what evidence is available.

Tools such as questionnaires, observation schedules and scales are developed in order to measure concepts and indicators. These tools are pre-determined, structured and standardised, in order to obtain standard responses to facilitate data analysis. They may measure extent, frequency, amount, number, prevalence, incidence, trends, patterns and relationships. They are administered in a standardised form, so that data are collected in a standardised fashion from all respondents.

Due to the positivist influenced reductionist element of quantitative research, in the same way that scientists reduce matter to atoms, there is a need for researchers to reduce or dissect the key components of each concept which relates to the research question. However, this is not always straightforward. For example, if we wish to demonstrate a relationship between high productivity and job satisfaction in a factory, it might be easy to define what high productivity means and to break it down and measure it in a numerical, scientific way (Yates 1998). However, what does the concept of job-satisfaction really mean and how do we measure it? Is job satisfaction based on how happy we are with what we earn, how we are treated, our working environment, our hours of work, or our perceived level of autonomy? There is no simple answer, yet attempts are made to find the best indicators or proxy measures for those concepts which are not directly measurable (Yates 1998).

Another aspect of operationalising our concepts is operationalising or defining our terminology. The importance of this in developing our research question has already been noted in the previous chapter. Furthermore, it is possible to identify different dimensions, aspects or facets of a concept, such as in the above example of job satisfaction. However, while there are potential difficulties of measurement, the definition of job satisfaction is relatively straightforward. Other concepts, such as professional competence, represent less tangible constructs. Indeed, competent health and social care practice requires complex combinations of knowledge, performance, skills, values and attitudes (Cowan, Norman & Coopamah 2005). Therefore, an integrated, holistic conception of competence in health and social care is required which incorporates professional judgement and involves complex activities, bringing together the different attributes and tasks required for intelligent performance (Cowan, Norman & Coopamah 2005). In order to measure such a complex multi-dimensional concept it is necessary to have a multi-dimensional tool which can capture the complexities of the concept.

In quantitative research, clear definition of terms is particularly pertinent to the study design, for example in the design of questionnaire surveys whereby our questions need to have the same meaning for each respondent. We need to consider what a certain concept may mean in everyday language. For example, what does competence mean in everyday use? Is it merely the opposite of incompetence or is it something that sits on a spectrum ranging from novice to competent to expert? As noted above, once again we need to take apart key elements in reductionist fashion in order to devise not only our measurement scale but our definition of a term.

As noted, a number of different tools which utilise various scales are available to capture and measure our concepts. These scales can be broadly categorised according to level of measurement, based on the type of information or data that they are intended to collect. These are:

Nominal Scales: Nominal scales are based on categorisation of data, for example, being positive or negative for a test, being male or female, being a smoker or non-smoker. Nominal categories have no defined order.

Ordinal Scales: Ordinal scales are based on categories that can be ordered or ranked, the categories can be located on a continuum, such as a pain rating scale from 0 to 10 (where 0 = no pain and 10 = worst pain), or risk classification such as: Low, Medium, High.

Interval Scales: Interval scales are based on a standardised unit of measurement but may not have an absolute zero, such as in temperature measurement.

Ratio Scales: Ratio scales have an absolute zero and enable exact comparisons, for example, one litre is twice the amount of half a litre.

The different types of data and subsequent level of measurement will influence the analysis and reporting of findings. However, ratio and interval data are usually treated in the same way with regard to statistical testing and reporting. Nominal and ordinal data, perceived as being at a lower level, are subjected to far more stringent statistical testing because they are not seen as being so robust. However, despite this, whether concepts are directly or indirectly measurable does not always have an influence on the level of data that can be collected. For example, being positive or negative for a scientifically applied biological test, the result of which can be directly and totally objectively measured, only yields nominal data, yet this is a direct, objective measurement. Conversely, measuring a person's pain with a pain rating scale from 0 to 10, yields ordinal data which can be rated on a scale, yet this is an indirect, subjective measurement. Incidentally, with regard to pain rating scores, we cannot say these are interval data, because the scale is 'made up' and cannot be described as having fixed intervals and we cannot say these are ratio data because we cannot determine if a person reporting a pain score of 10 is in twice as much pain as a person reporting a score of 5. The point is however, that in using only an indirect, subjective, proxy measure for a variable, we have generated data that is seen as more robust than data collected by direct, objective measurement.

In the same way, it would be possible to collect ratio data in the form of number of years working since qualifying as a professional and use this as a proxy measure for job experience. However, it may be the case that somebody working in a less busy unit for a long period may be less experienced than a person working in a very busy unit for a short period. Once again, despite this, because ten years' experience is exactly twice the amount of five years' experience, in theory, the data collected could be seen as more robust than nominal or ordinal data and be subject to less rigorous statistical testing, when in fact it may be less accurate than the other two levels of data. These examples serve to contradict the idea that purely objective measures can be considered as more reliable than subjective indicators or proxy measures.

Variables

Variables

When measuring variations in a given concept, such as an increase or decrease in the level of something, such as weight, particularly in experimental studies, concepts are described as 'variables'. Variables may be in the form of a substance, such as a type of food or a drug; they may be of physical nature such as height or weight; they may be physiological, such as blood pressure or heart rate; they may be psychological, such as anxiety or depression; they may be social, such as education or occupation; they may be behavioural such as smoking or drinking and some fall within more than one area and may be multi-dimensional such as in the above example of professional competence.

Variables can then be further described as being either dependent or independent. The dependent variable is also known as the outcome variable and the independent variable influences or affects the dependent variable. For example, if the variables being measured in an experiment on lowering blood pressure are blood pressure among people with high blood pressure and a drug developed to lower high blood pressure, the dependent (or outcome) variable would be blood pressure and the drug intended to lower blood pressure would be the independent variable. Thus, blood pressure would not be expected to have an effect on the drug, but the drug would be expected to have an effect on blood pressure.

Hypotheses

Hypotheses

In conducting an experiment on lowering blood pressure, clearly we would have some kind of theory to begin with, whereby we anticipated that a particular drug could lower blood pressure. As stated earlier, while quantitative research does not always entail having a hypothesis, when conducting an experiment it is seen as standard practice to start with a theory and from this theory to generate a hypothesis. Thus, we use the general claims of the theory to make precise statements about the effect of one variable (the independent variable) on another (the dependent variable) (Yates 1998). Using the abovementioned experiment, our hypothesis might be that drug x will lower blood pressure by a predetermined amount – usually the mean average blood pressure in a group of people (averages will be returned to in the following chapter), as measured by a predetermined scale – in the case of blood pressure, usually millimetres of mercury. Using the deductive approach we then test our hypothesis with our experiment.

As noted in the previous chapter, if we have a hypothesis that a particular intervention can improve a particular condition, in this case high blood pressure, when we design our study we are not designing it to prove that our hypothesis is correct, we are seeking to suggest that we are not wrong. In order to support this suggestion of not being wrong, we need to be able to reject the null hypothesis (H0) which is a competing hypothesis stating that our drug x to lower blood pressure will not work and that any positive effects will be due to chance rather than the properties of the drug – that the high blood pressure would have lowered with time anyway. The alternative hypothesis (H1) is that drug x will lower blood pressure.

If our study findings indicate that we can reject the null hypothesis, this does not mean that our hypothesis (the alternative hypothesis H1) is correct without question, it means that it is supported. This process is described as falsificationist and was first proposed by Sir Karl Popper (1902–1994) who advocated that it was unscientific to continually seek to verify a hypothesis, in the way that so-called logical positivists had been doing, because it only takes a single instance of falsification to disprove numerous instances of verification. This process also became known as the post-positivist approach.

However, as also noted in the previous chapter, we have to recognise that we can never be 100% sure that the findings are true because there is always the possibility that our results are due to chance. Therefore, statistical testing of the significance of our results is used to determine the likelihood of our results being due to chance. Conventionally, we do not accept our results as statistically significant unless there is a probability of less than 5% that they could be due to chance. This is expressed as a 'p' value of 0.05, written as: $p < 0.05$. So if our test of statistical significance tells us that the probability of our findings being due to chance is higher than 5%, in this case we would say that our hypothesis is not supported and therefore we cannot reject the 'null hypothesis' whereby we have to accept that drug x did not lower blood pressure in our experiment ('p' values will be returned to in later chapters).

As stated earlier, while in quantitative research the deductive approach usually dominates, in that researchers select in advance which variables they will investigate and state their hypothesis to be tested, sometimes an experiment can discover something not widely known or recognised previously. For example, a side-effect of some anti-depressant drugs is that they also have pain-killing properties. In this case, our experiment would be generating a new theory and a subsequent hypothesis to be tested and could therefore be described as an inductive process.

As also noted earlier, a key assumption of positivism is that scientific laws can be found, with empirical regularities seen as providing the basis for this and statistical tests telling us the probability of a regularity being due to random chance (Yates 1998). While results of studies may modify theories, predictions and hypotheses, it should be noted that in some cases, a non-significant result may prompt the researcher to decide not to change their hypothesis, but instead to improve the study design until a significant result is obtained (Yates 1998).

Validity and reliability

Validity and reliability

In addition to developing measurements in order to test hypotheses, quantitative research often involves testing these measurements for their validity and reliability. Validity pertains to the degree to which a measure actually measures what it purports to be measuring. Face or content validity is concerned with whether the measure is relevant to the characteristics of the concept being measured. Face or content validation usually occurs during the development of a measure and is typically undertaken via a consensus of expert opinion. Criterion validation is concerned with whether a measure will predict a later trend or pattern of characteristics (predictive), whether a measure will isolate a known characteristic (post-dictive) and whether a measure will demonstrate or isolate a characteristic as confirmed by concurrently conducted tests for other criteria that are known to be related to the characteristic (concurrent). Construct validation involves examining the internal consistency of a measure, for example to determine if the elements within a measure of a multi-dimensional concept are appropriately related according to a statistical test such as Cronbach's Alpha. Discriminal validity is concerned with how sensitive and specific a measure is. For example, a test may be sensitive enough to identify everybody with a particular condition, with a 100 % success rate. However, it may be so sensitive as to wrongly identify people as having the condition as well. In this case the test would be described as highly sensitive in picking up all the true positives but not very specific in that it also picks up a lot of false positives. Overall then, validity is particularly concerned with the accuracy of a measure.

If validity is concerned with the overall accuracy of a measure, then reliability is concerned with the overall consistency of a measure. Reliability testing is generally concerned with four basic types of consistency: consistency between parallel tests whereby the results of a different test for the same characteristic will be correlated, consistency across time whereby the results of a test will be correlated with the results of the test taken by the same respondents at a different time (it should be remembered that the respondent's characteristics may change over time), consistency between raters whereby two different researchers administer a measure and the results are correlated for consistency and internal consistency, whereby the same procedure for assessing construct validity is undertaken.

While validity and reliability are related, there are differences. Importantly, it should be remembered it is possible to have a measure that is reliable but not valid, because a test can be consistently wrong and consistently wrong by the same amount, a bit like consistently firing a gun through a sighting device that you think is accurate but that is consistently off target by exactly the same distance with each shot. However, it is not possible to have a valid test that is not reliable, because it could not then be considered as accurate.

Measures that are used in quantitative research may not always be tested for validity and reliability, usually due to lack of resources including time and money. This does not mean that these measures are inaccurate or inconsistent, just that these aspects are not known. If validity and reliability testing is not mentioned in research reports then it can be assumed that this has not been undertaken.

Some examples of quantitative research designs

Questionnaire surveys

Questionnaire surveys

The questionnaire survey is a commonly used design in quantitative research. It has several advantages including: flexibility of when and where it can be administered – it does not usually need to be undertaken in strictly controlled environments such as a laboratory or clinical setting, no physical intervention is required and it is usually administered relatively quickly (as opposed to experiments that may take hours, days or weeks) thereby making it more amenable to potential respondents and easier to convince people to participate in and it is capable of generating large amounts of data relative to the resources and efforts of the researcher or research team that are employed.

Questionnaire surveys may be interactive, that is, completed in 'face to face' fashion where the researcher asks the respondent questions directly or by telephone and fills in the answers. Interactive completion can be costly and may introduce bias in the form of respondents' reactivity to the person asking the questions, but may be useful if the respondent requires clarification from the researcher about the questions. Alternatively, questionnaires may be self-completed by respondents, this may be more appropriate in some circumstances, such as in the case of questions being asked about sensitive subjects. However, if questionnaires are sent out by post, the response rate is not usually as good as when prospective respondents are approached in person by the researcher.

As noted earlier in this chapter, in operationalising our terminology, we need to ensure that wherever possible the words and questions that are used have fixed meanings. Other considerations in designing a survey relate to the prior knowledge that the respondent is likely to hold – will they be able to understand and answer the questions? Also, are there too many questions? Do all of the questions have relevance or are they there because they seemed like a good idea at the time? Remember, people may get questionnaire fatigue and become bored with filling it in and stop. It is also useful to consider what the motivation of respondents may be; for example, is this a good opportunity for people to complain about something, thereby providing the researcher with biased results in that only those with a grudge to bear bothered to respond to the survey.

The type of questioning used may be direct, such as, how old are you, or how long have you been employed for? Questions may be two-way, such as male or female, yes or no; they may be in multiple choice format, or they may be scaled as in strongly agree, agree, don't know, disagree, strongly disagree. The latter format is often referred to as a Likert scale (Likert 1932).

Surveys may be cross-sectional in that they take a 'snap shot' of what is current; they may be retrospective in that the respondent is asked to recall something (this could be hampered by forgetfulness and/or 'hindsight bias'), or they may be prospective in that respondents will be asked a series of questions across time. It is also feasible to conduct a comparative survey in which the responses to a set of questions of two or more distinct groups are compared for similarities or differences. In this way it is possible to design and conduct a hypothesis-testing survey. For example, if we have a theory that a particular social group is disadvantaged in that they are perceived as less able to access a particular social service, we can generate a hypothesis to this effect and then test it through their responses to questions, as compared to a group that is perceived as more able to access the particular service in question.

A number of different types of questionnaire survey are commonly in general use at any one time including: consumer surveys, service user satisfaction surveys, opinion polls, crime surveys and the national census. These can be used to inform us of what the current opinions, attitudes, behaviours, beliefs, values, preferences, dislikes, ideas and various prevalences and trends are, and the findings can be utilised to make predictions for the future and to make appropriate service provision.

General disadvantages of questionnaire surveys are that the findings are often superficial, we cannot usually infer cause or effect from the findings (this is often true of experiments as well and will be returned to), despite being easier to conduct than most experiments, some surveys can be time-consuming, particularly if there is a problem of non-response and questionnaires have had to be redistributed on several occasions in order to collect enough data.

Experiments

Experiments commonly measure the effect of one variable (independent variable) on another (dependent variable) or less commonly they may merely observe participants in a particular setting. In fact, experiments that can be classified as observational as opposed to interventional usually involve observing somebody or something in a particular experimental setting. Thus, deliberately placing somebody or something in a particular setting can be defined as applying an intervention, as opposed to a purely observational study such as in ethnographic studies, where participants are observed and studied in their natural surroundings (ethnography will be discussed in more detail in Chapter 6 on qualitative research). Most experiments are concerned with assessing the effectiveness of an intervention, the intervention being the independent variable and the effect being the measured change in the dependent variable.

Randomised controlled trial

As noted in Chapter 2, the randomised controlled trial (RCT) and systematic reviews or meta-analyses of RCTs are seen by some as the 'gold standard' for judging whether an intervention does more good than harm and have become the hallmark of experimental testing (Sackett 1996, Haynes 2002). (Systematic reviews and meta-analyses will be returned to in Chapters 5 and 9.) In a RCT participants are randomly allocated in order to avoid bias of selection, for example to stop a person choosing which group they wanted to be in, to either a control (normal) group (which has an existing intervention or no intervention), or an intervention (study) group (which has the intervention to be tested). The groups must be well-matched to avoid bias, for example, the people in one group should not be considerably older than in the other group. Furthermore, if the mindset of the researcher who generated the hypothesis and designed the experiment favours the effectiveness of the intervention being tested, then their assessment of the outcomes may be subconsciously biased in favour of the intervention. To avoid such bias, the assessor of the outcomes can be 'blinded' as to whether the participants they are assessing are from the control group or intervention group, or another 'neutral' person can undertake the assessments.

In order to prevent participants being convinced by the power of suggestion (also known as the 'placebo' effect, which, incidentally is poorly understood) that because they are having an intervention to improve their condition they must they feel better, it may also be possible to 'blind' the participants as to whether they are in the control or treatment group. This is usually easier in drug studies. Using the example of an experiment to test a drug that is thought to lower blood pressure, we could have a control group which takes an existing drug known to lower blood pressure (normal or existing intervention) and a study group which takes a new drug thought to be more effective in lowering blood pressure. Both groups are given the drugs in tablet form and the tablets comprising both drugs have been made to look exactly the same in order to 'blind' the participants as to what intervention they are actually having. The results for both groups are then statistically analysed and compared to determine if there was a significant difference in outcome (lowered blood pressure) between the groups (as stated, analysis of quantitative research data will be discussed in more detail in the next chapter). A variation of this approach would be to give the control group a 'dummy' tablet which has no effect on blood pressure and in this way separate out the 'placebo' effect from the actual effect of the intervention, which in some studies can be as high as 20–40% of respondents reporting an improved outcome after being given a 'dummy' drug (the figure of 20–40% is based on the author's experience).

When the assessor is blinded, this is known as a single blind study, when both assessor and participants are blinded this is known as a double-blind study. Thus, in testing the effectiveness of an intervention, the most robust type of experimental design would be a double-blind RCT.

Cross-over design

Instead of having two separate parallel groups it is possible to conduct an RCT using the same group twice, who 'cross-over', first having participants in the study group and then crossing over into the control group or vice versa, randomly allocating them as to which group they go into first. The attraction of the cross-over design is that of 'within person comparison' whereby we can observe the intervention effect compared to the control effect in the same person, enabling the direct comparison of effects which may be more precise, as opposed to relying on data derived from two different effects in two different people, which may vary due to individual personal preference. Also, using the same group twice means that only half of the number of participants is needed compared to a parallel group design, saving on recruitment time and other resources. Cross-over studies are only appropriate when the condition under examination will not be permanently changed by the intervention provided in the first phase of the study. Furthermore, there are some drawbacks of the cross-over design as opposed to the parallel group design. The risk of people dropping out (sample attrition) of the study would be doubled compared to a parallel group study, as people who dropped out of one group would be effectively dropping out of both groups. If a 'blinded' participant recognises treatment, therefore becoming 'unblinded' in the first period of a cross-over study, they will definitely know which treatment they are having in the second period. This would not be the case in a parallel group study. Also, there may be logistical problems with regard to a 'carry over' effect whereby participants who were crossing over groups were still experiencing the effects of the first intervention and unable to distinguish this from the second intervention. To avoid this, cross-over studies may need to have a 'wash-out' period in between study groups, which will cause additional delay in completion of the experiment.

Quasi-Experiments

There are other types of quantitative research study which are not as rigorous as the RCT, whereby one or more requirements for classification as an RCT are missing, for example, studies in which randomisation to study groups does not take place. These are generally known as 'quasi -experiments'. There are quasi-experimental studies that employ what is known as a 'pre-post' design whereby participants are in a single group which is measured before and after an intervention. Again using the example of blood pressure, in a pre-post intervention study design, a single group of people with high blood pressure would have their blood pressure recorded as a baseline measure, they would be given a drug to lower their blood pressure for a fixed period of time and then their blood pressure would be measured again to compare for differences between their pre and post test condition, which can then be statistically analysed for significance.

Advantages and disadvantages of experiments

General advantages of experiments are that they, particularly RCTs, can provide high quality information and can be deterministic – thinking back to the cause versus effect dichotomy, experiments can often tell us if our interventions have been the cause of the desired effect. Furthermore, with regard to the notion of causality, experiments often do not merely describe, they can provide us with an explanation beyond a mere association between two variables. Thus, from an experiment it is possible to infer cause and effect – that one thing causes another. Also, for experiments, because of the degree of closure and control that is exercised, such as through objective measurement utilised to reduce bias, often, smaller sample sizes are required to produce statistically significant results. Some general disadvantages of experiments are that they can be expensive, complex and time-consuming, so we cannot employ as large numbers of participants as for other types of study such as questionnaire surveys. Also, experimental control and closure may eliminate the 'real world' factor and such experiments may not permit the description of the total experience of participants.

Other types of quantitative study

In addition to questionnaire surveys, there are other types of non-experimental, descriptive quantitative research studies. Case control studies are used to compare two groups of people. One group comprises people with a particular condition under study (the cases) and a similar group comprises people without the condition (the controls). The lifestyles and histories of each group are then studied in order to determine which factors could be associated with the condition. For example, it may transpire that one group may have been exposed to a particular substance or environment to which the other was not exposed. This is also known as a retrospective study.

Cohort studies are undertaken to observe a particular group of people (the cohort), across time in order to determine what happens to them. For example, a particular group of graduate social workers or nurses might be followed throughout their working lives to determine how many of them actually stay within their chosen profession and for how long. This is also known as a prospective or longitudinal study.

Quantitative research methods

Case series studies are undertaken to collect and analyse data from a series of 'cases', these cases usually based on individual people, in order to determine various trends and/or prevalences. Case studies are also associated with a qualitative research approach but can be quantitative in nature, such as in the case of a large organisation being evaluated and thus yielding considerable quantities of data.

There can be certain advantages to non-experimental types of quantitative study. While experiments can be more reliable in inferring that one thing causes another, prior to experimentation we often do not know which way around the relationship is. For example a questionnaire survey of heroin users may find that 100% of people who are dependent on heroin and injecting it several times daily, started by smoking heroin only occasionally. We might then hypothesise that, 100% of the time, people who started out occasionally smoking heroin end up becoming dependent on it and injecting it. But it would be difficult, not to mention unethical to design an experiment to test this hypothesis. We could however design a longitudinal cohort study to observe across time a cohort of people who occasionally smoke heroin to determine how many of these might become heroin-dependent injectors. There may be other factors involved in becoming dependent on heroin, such as a person's life history, for example, being abused as a child. In order to discover these aspects we could design a retrospective case control study with two groups of people, one group of people dependent on heroin (the cases) and one group that does not use heroin (the controls). We could then examine the lifestyles and histories of each group in order to determine which factors could be associated with becoming dependent on heroin.

Terminology box

Quantitative methods
- Systematic reviews/Meta-analysis of RCTs (please see Chapters 5 and 9)
- Randomised controlled trials (RCT)
- Quasi experiments – pre-post test
- Observational studies: Case control/Cohort
- Surveys.

Sampling techniques for quantitative research

Sampling techniques

Sampling refers to the process of selecting participants for experiments and studies, or selecting respondents to questionnaire surveys. Sampling can represent a form of statistical closure in research because whoever is in the sample determines what data we can collect and analyse.

However, we need to be able say that our findings can be generalised beyond the confines of the particular context in which research was conducted and that our results can apply to individuals other than those that participated in the study. Indeed, Bryman (2004) cites generalisation as one of the main features of quantitative research. Therefore, if quantitative research is to produce findings which are truly generalisable, then we need to draw what can be deemed as 'representative' samples from the population that we wish to study, as usually we do not have the time and resources to study the whole population in question. The term 'population' does not just mean the whole population of the UK, but could mean for example, the whole population of heroin users in the UK. Therefore, if we designed a study of heroin users to find out how much heroin they consumed every week, if we were using just a sample of them, we would need to be able to generalise our findings from that sample to the whole population of heroin users. Thus, we would need to ensure that our sample was representative. There would be no point in studying only people who occasionally smoked heroin as this sample would be biased and they would not provide the same data as those users who regularly injected heroin.

Probability sampling

One of the techniques employed to try and ensure that we get a representative sample is known as probability sampling. Probability sampling involves randomly selecting participants to be studied in order to avoid bias. Thus, in simple random sampling whereby we could draw people's names from a hat (computer programmes can now do the equivalent for us), everybody has an equal chance of being selected. In stratified random sampling we ensure that each strata of conditions or status is adequately represented, such as ensuring that people of all age groups are represented. Systematic random sampling entails selecting every nth number on a list – for example every third person. Cluster random sampling means that we randomly select units such as a number of hospitals and then either study everyone in them or randomly select people from them for study.

Non-probability sampling

The alternative to probability sampling is non-probability sampling. Indeed, in reality it is not always possible to use probability sampling; as in the case of the population of heroin users in the UK, it would not be feasible to select a random sample from them because we do not know who they all are, particularly those who are not registered with any kind of drug treatment facility. Parahoo (2006) describes two broad and overlapping categories of non-probability sampling – purposive/judgemental sampling which involves some choice and judgement, thus a degree of control, and convenience sampling which entails whoever is available being chosen. In practice however the distinction is not rigid as both types of sampling method may involve a degree of judgement and convenience (Parahoo 2006).

Convenience sampling is quite often used in both quantitative and qualitative research. Certainly if we wanted to study heroin users we might have to make do with whoever we could find who was cooperative enough to participate in a study. If we did find people who were cooperative we may ask them if they know anybody else who would be interested in participating – this is known as snowball sampling, whereby a respondent refers someone to the study, they refer someone else and so on. Volunteer sampling refers to research where people respond to an advert inviting them to participate; this method is commonly used by drug companies (or their contract research companies) to recruit members of the public on to clinical drug trials. However, sometimes a 'captive' population, such as a group of hospital patients or a class of students may be invited to participate in some research, although there are ethical implications in coercing people to participate (the subject of research ethics will be discussed in more detail in Chapter 11). Accidental sampling usually refers to the process of interviewing people in the street, such as when a researcher stands in a shopping mall in order to undertake a piece of market research.

Sample size estimation and calculation

One of the questions often asked of tutors by students and of statisticians by researchers is:

'How large should my sample be?' Unfortunately there is not always an easy answer to this question, particularly with regard to survey research. As a general rule, one can say that the larger the sample is, the more likely it is to be representative of the population being studied. For example, if our target population is known to be 1000 people, studying just 10 of them would not be as useful as studying 300.

However, calculation of sample sizes is possible if we know the size of the difference we are looking for. That may be the difference between responses from two groups of people who are surveyed or it may be the difference in effect of an intervention used in an experiment. This is known as the effect size (ES) and the bigger the difference we are looking for, the easier it will be to detect, thus requiring a smaller sample. Returning to the example of blood pressure and drug x, if we know how much we want drug x to lower the mean average blood pressure in a group of people, say by at least 30%, as compared to another group who are not given drug x, then we can calculate the numbers of people required for each group, allowing for a degree of error in the statistical significance, remembering that we accept we cannot be 100% certain.

The ES is calculated by dividing the desired difference between mean averages by the standard deviation (SD) of the means. Determining the size of the SD involves calculating the difference from the mean average of each individual value in the data set, squaring each value, adding them all together, dividing the total by the number of values in the data set and then calculating the square root of that figure. (Standard deviations will be returned to in the following chapter.)

Calculating the effect size: example

$$ES = \frac{\text{desired difference in means}}{\text{standard deviation (SD)}}$$

If mean systolic blood pressure is 180 (SD 3.8), you may decide to try and reduce this by at least 30% (54)

Therefore:

$$ES = \frac{54}{3.8} = 14.2 \text{ (then look up this value on the chart)}$$

So, imagine that we plan to study two groups of people, both with an average blood pressure of 180, one group having drug x and the other group having a placebo and we want to be able to detect at least a 30% reduction in blood pressure between them after drug x and the placebo have been given, but we do not know how many people to have in each group. The chart below shows us how many people we would need in each group, dependent on the effect size.

For an effect size of 2 or above (and 14.2 is well above 2) we would only need six people in each group. This is because a 30% difference is relatively large and therefore easier to detect and therefore requires a relatively small sample size. However, in the unlikely event of deciding that we want to be able to detect a difference of only 1% then we would divide 1.8 (1% of 180) by the SD of 3.8 giving us 0.47 and we can see on the chart below that this is higher than 0.4 so we would need two groups of 135 people to detect this difference between the groups.

Methods: estimating sample size:
Power chart for *t*-test

Effect size	$p < 0.05$ @ 90% power n per group
2	6
1.5	11
1.2	16
1	22

Effect Size	p < 0.05 @ 90% power n per group
0.8	35
0.6	60
0.4	135
0.3	240
0.2	550

Sample size: estimating prevalence: examples

Another way of calculating a sample size is based on estimating the prevalence of a particular phenomenon that you wish to detect, for example, a condition or an attitude. Below are some examples of calculations that can be undertaken using a computer programme, which is available as a free 10-day download from: www.statsdirect.co.uk. You can use Statsdirect for many other statistical calculations, although after 10 days you will be required to buy the programme software otherwise it will stop working.

- To detect 20% prevalence plus/minus 5% @ 95% confidence, in a population of 50, minimum sample required = 42

- To detect 20% prevalence plus/minus 5% @ 95% confidence, in a population of 100, minimum sample required = 72

- To detect 20% prevalence plus/minus 5% @ 95% confidence, in a population of 1000, minimum sample required = 198

- To detect 20% prevalence plus/minus 5% @ 95% confidence, in a population of 5000, minimum sample required = 235

Sample size: considerations

Furthermore, it should be remembered that determining your sample size usually represents a compromise between:

- resources
- time
- cost
- need for precision
- availability of participants.

The bigger the sample, the more likely it is to be representative of the general population.

Criticisms of quantitative research

Criticisms of quantitative research

There are several general criticisms of quantitative research, some of which have been noted in this chapter, with regard to problems in classification and analysis of data, and others which have already been highlighted in Chapter 2. Quantitative research is criticised by many qualitative researchers and these criticisms revolve around the view that the natural science model of research is appropriate for studying the social world and that only the scientific method can produce knowledge worthy of being called hard evidence (Yates 1998).

Parahoo (2006) notes the limitations of quantitative research in understanding human phenomena and behaviour – we can only study what is observable, we cannot always observe and measure concepts such as: stress, hope, love, emotion and anxiety. Furthermore, we cannot understand deeper meanings that different people attach to concepts by asking questions that require a standardised 'fixed' response, because these items can be interpreted differently (Parahoo 2006). Indeed, selecting questions to include in questionnaire surveys and in structured interviews is not a value-free, neutral exercise, they are informed by theoretical, philosophical justification and the beliefs, values and assumptions of researchers are incorporated (Parahoo 2006). Thus, what appears to be objectivity reflects the values of the researchers and may not reflect the thoughts and values of service users (Parahoo 2006). Furthermore in the search for objectivity, what is perceived as the undue influence of external factors is often closed out – however, it may be contested as to what constitutes undue influence or what may be merely a 'real world effect' whereby life actually involves a degree of unavoidable subjectivity. Once again, we are confronted with the objectivity versus subjectivity dichotomy.

Despite their attempts to mirror natural science, such as with techniques for sampling and analysis of data, truly positivist assumptions are not conformed with by quantitative researchers (Yates 1998). For example, while beliefs, feelings and values are subjective, attempts are still made to measure these. Also, quantitative researchers have had to address the issue of meaning and placed human activity and behaviour within the realm of meaning. However, this requires specific research methods which deal with this and they are often qualitative in nature.

It should be remembered that systematic reviews and meta-analyses can be biased in that only certain studies are included in the review, for example papers in English only, or papers that are included based on the opinion of a single judge of the quality of papers. Also, it is not possible to undertake a systematic review if not enough primary studies of good quality have been published. Furthermore, there may be publication bias, where not all studies have been published. Indeed, studies showing a significant effect of something are more likely to be published. If peer reviewers for a journal reject a study that has unfavourable results, then the authors may not be so keen to resubmit, whereas with a study with significant, favourable results they may be more likely to persevere.

Parahoo (2006) states that if quantitative data could be taken at face value and not what they pretend to be, then not so much criticism would be levelled at quantitative research. Parahoo (2006) believes that it is not data in themselves that are pretentious, just the claim that they provide hard evidence which elevates quantitative research to a level far above others, this being a highly contested position.

Bryman (2004) notes the gap between ideal and actual research practice, the main steps in the quantitative research process being of an ideal and typical nature, but rarely found in this pure form. Furthermore, teachers of research cannot cover every eventuality, therefore they tend to draw upon common features. Thus, the quantitative research process should be seen as a general tendency, rather than a definitive description (Bryman 2004). Bryman (2004) notes further the need for teachers and researchers to provide an account of good practice in research, but this is often not found in the published research papers that students encounter. This failure is usually associated with lack of time, cost and feasibility – many of these being pragmatic concerns that cannot be avoided. However, in addition, researchers often make inferences beyond their selected sample. Despite this, even when they do not, the quantitative process is dependent on results that either support or refute a claim to truth, yet we can not rely on these methods to the point where we can be 100% sure.

Quantitative research methods

As was noted in Chapter 2, Parahoo (2006) observes that in the last two decades other approaches have been challenging and stating their own claims to production of knowledge. Accordingly, the qualitative approach will be discussed in Chapters 6 and 7 on qualitative research methods and analysis of qualitative data.

Conclusion

Despite criticisms, quantitative research is valuable and important in health and social care. Indeed, as Parahoo (2006) notes, quantitative research studies are still the favoured approach for those who provide funding for research and as Grypdonck (2006) notes, this is not likely to change in the near future. The findings of quantitative research can be used to predict outcomes, leading to the prevention of undesirable ones, also in identifying trends, patterns, prevalence, attitudes, needs, roles, activities, satisfaction, beliefs, competence, service delivery and organisation, testing and evaluation of new interventions and comparison with existing ones. Surveys can provide large amounts of data in a short period of time and are relatively cost-effective. Quantitative research findings can inform policy decisions and justify expenditure. Thus, despite challenges in recent decades from qualitative quarters, since the introduction of EBP, quantitative research has gained a new impetus and proliferated (Parahoo 2006).

The following chapter examines some techniques utilised in the analysis of quantitative research data.

Chapter 5
Analysis of quantitative data

Introduction

This chapter deals with the analysis of data derived from quantitative research studies. As with the last chapter on quantitative research, it should be noted that this chapter will not detail all types of quantitative data analysis, just some of the main, commonly used types. In examining the treatment of quantitative research data, we will consider how such data can be described, represented, summarised and analysed using statistical methods. You will be introduced to measures of central tendency (averages), measures of spread, different levels of data, some statistical testing of data, including significance testing and how to interpret results.

Statistical analyses are useful in reducing large data sets down to a manageable form. Data are usually represented by numbers and as mentioned in the previous chapter, different types of data are generated via quantitative research, these being:

- nominal
- ordinal
- interval
- ratio.

Accordingly there are a number of different ways of analysing these data. Parametric tests are applied when data are at least interval level, normally distributed – that is, when the standard deviation is not very high and at least 68% of the values are within plus or minus one standard deviation of the mean average – and thus the mean average is a true representation of the central value (mean averages and standard deviations will be returned to later in this chapter). Non-parametric tests are applied when data do not meet requirements of parametric statistics and are used to analyse data at nominal and ordinal levels.

There are also several different types of analysis: univariate, bivariate and multivariate.

Univariate

Univariate

Univariate data are usually at the descriptive level of data interpretation and as the term suggests, data are merely described. This may be in the form of a single percentage (as in a holiday company stating that 99% of holidaymakers said they would travel with the company again), or as the central value – the average (for example, as in average earnings) and the distribution of values around the average. There are three types of average – the **mean**, **median** and **mode**. The mean average, which is sensitive to all values, is calculated by adding together all of the values in a data set and then dividing the total by the number of values.

Thus, the mean average for the following data set comprising ten values: 1,2,2,3,3,3,3,4,4,5
would be: $\dfrac{1+2+2+3+3+3+3+4+4+5}{10} = \dfrac{30}{10} = 3$

The median average is the midpoint in the data set $1,2,2,3,3\Downarrow3,3,4,4,5 = 3$, and the mode average is the most frequently occurring value, which in this dataset would again be 3.

However, it should be remembered that the mean, median and mode for the same data set may all be different, as demonstrated in the following data set: 1,2,2,2,3,3,4,4,5,10. The mean would be 3.6, the median would be 5 and the mode would be 2.

It should also be remembered that the mean average can be influenced by extreme values, so if we had a data set with very high or very low outlying values this would disproportionately increase or decrease the mean average. The median average represents the midpoint and is a useful measure of central tendency. The mode tells us the most frequently occurring value. However, all three types of average can provide useful information about a data set.

If there is no true midpoint such as in the following data set: 1,2,2,2,2,2,4,4,4,4,4,5 then it is necessary to take the middle two values, add them together and divide them by two, therefore in this case the midpoint (median) would be: $\dfrac{2 + 4}{2} = 3$

If two modal values exist, as in the above data set (2 and 4), then a single mode average value cannot be calculated.

When reporting descriptive statistics, we can calculate measures of spread (distribution) around our central values (or averages) in order to portray how accurate our central value actually is.

Commonly used measures of spread are: the range (useful with all three types of average), the standard deviation (a measure of variance) useful only with the mean average and the inter-quartile range.

The range measures the spread between the highest and lowest values, so in reporting these values for the above data sets the ranges are typically written as 1–5, 1–10 and 1–5 respectively.

The standard deviation (SD) as noted in the previous chapter, involves calculating the difference from the mean average of each individual value in the data set, squaring each value, adding them all together, dividing the total by the number of values in the data set and then calculating the square root of that figure. Fortunately, computer programmes are now available to do these calculations, once a data set has been entered into a spreadsheet. The rule is that the larger the range and standard deviation are, the less accurate the mean average is and vice versa.

Going back to our example of data on blood pressure, we can see from the figures below that all of the blood pressure values in the data set are quite close to the mean average, indicating that the mean average is quite accurate and that this is represented by a relatively small SD.

180, 175, 178, 177, 182, 185, 186, 179, 181, 175
Mean average = 179.8, SD = 3.8

The inter-quartile range is useful in that it is not influenced by extraordinary high or low outlying values in a data set. The inter-quartile range is calculated by first splitting the data into half by calculating the median and then further splitting the two halves into quarters by again calculating the midpoints. The inter-quartile range is then calculated as the difference between the lower and higher quartiles, that is taking the range as the middle two quartiles.

Example of consideration of different types of central value

If we look at the example of two imaginary companies' reports of the mean average earnings of their employees we can appreciate the use of the distribution of values around the central value and also the use of considering the different types of central value in informing us as to the accuracy of certain claims.

Company One reports mean average earnings for their employees as £29,100 per year and Company Two reports mean average earnings for their employees as £34,500 per year. It would appear then that Company Two is the better company to work for, from the point of view of earning a better salary anyway. However, when we look at the ranges and standard deviations around the mean averages in Table 5.1, we can tell that in Company Two, the mean average does not appear to be a very representative figure of what people actually earn in that company.

Table 5.1

Comparison of mean averages

Company One		Company Two	
Mean	£29,100	Mean	£34,500
Range	£20,000 to £40,000	Range	£12,000 to £1.8 million
Standard Deviation	0.3	Standard Deviation	171.6

Looking at Table 5.2 below, we can confirm our suspicions. In Company One most people (90) do in fact earn close to the mean average of £29,100 per year and this is also represented in the mode and median values, whereas in Company Two, nobody earns close to the mean average of £34,500 per year, in fact the majority of people earn £20,000 or below; this is also represented in the mode and median values. The large standard deviation around the mean in Company Two should alert us to the fact that the mean is not very representative of the true average earnings in that company.

Table 5.2

Comparison of mode and median

Company One		Company Two	
No. of employees earning £20,000	10	No. of employees earning £12,000–£18,000	40
No. of employees earning £30,000	90	No. of employees earning £20,000	70
No. of employees earning £40,000	1	No. of employees earning £1.8 million	1
Mode	£30,000	Mode	£20,000
Median	£30,000	Median	£20,000

While the above examples may be somewhat simplistic and exaggerated, the important thing to remember is to be wary of a single figure presented as the 'average', accompanied by no further qualification or data.

Bivariate and multivariate

Bivariate and multivariate

When we have two data sets (bivariate data) we might want to compare them but we might also want to demonstrate a relationship between them. In such cases it is possible to do a correlation. This measures how close the relationship is between two values (variables). As the term suggests, we are now at the relational level of statistical analysis.

Table 5.3 gives some examples of tests for different types of correlation.

Table 5.3

Tests for correlation

Level of data	No. of variables	Test	Example of study
Ordinal (Non-parametric)	2	Spearman's rank order correlation	Relationship between depression and level of social class
Interval/Ratio (Parametric)	2	Pearson's rank correlation coefficient	Relationship between increasing blood pressure and age

Correlations measure two values from a continuous scale and are written as: 1 = a perfect positive correlation, 0 = no correlation, -1 = a perfect negative correlation. A positive correlation is when two variables move in the same direction, for example, blood pressure increasing as age increases. A negative correlation is when two variables move in different directions to each other, for example lung function test score diminishing as age increases.

However, it is not enough just to find a good correlation, even a perfect one, as we need to know the probability of it being due to random chance. It is easier to get a good correlation with smaller samples. We could easily demonstrate a perfect correlation of something in two people but would we be able to do the same with 200? Thus, we need to know if a perfect correlation of 1 between increasing blood pressure and age in a sample of five people is better than a correlation of 0.7 in a sample of 30 people. Looking up the level of significance in a table will tell us this.

Table 5.4　　**Significance table for Spearman's correlation**

Number of people in sample (n)	Level of Significance	
	$p < 0.05$	$p < 0.01$
5	0.90	1.00
10	0.56	0.75
20	0.38	0.53
30	0.31	0.43

Looking at Table 5.4 we can see that the level of significance for a perfect correlation of 1, in a sample of five people is $p < 0.01$ This means that there is less than a 1% likelihood of this correlation being due to chance. However, for a larger sample of 30 people we would only need a less than perfect correlation of 0.43, thus demonstrating that statistical testing is more rigorous for smaller samples because it is easier to demonstrate a correlation in such samples. Significance testing will be returned to later in this chapter.

It should be noted that correlations only show an association between variables, not which variable affects the other. For example, we might find a positive correlation between the amount of cannabis smoked and degree of mental illness. However, does smoking cannabis really make people mentally ill or does having mental illness predispose people to smoke cannabis? This is in fact an example of an ongoing debate which has yet to be concluded beyond doubt, despite strong arguments from various quarters.

There are literally hundreds of different statistical tests available for relating and comparing bivariate and multivariate (more than two data sets) data, which are too numerous to cover within the scope of this book. Therefore, it is only feasible to impart the underlying logic. However, it is important to know that we need to find the right type of statistical analysis or test for the type of data collected. Table 5.5 gives some examples of statistical tests for the statistical analysis of different types of data:

Table 5.5　　**Examples of statistical tests for different types of data**

Level of data	No. of groups	No. of categories	Test	Example of study
Nominal	1	2	McNemar (Binomial) test	A study to determine whether there are equal numbers of males and females in a group attending a drug detoxification programme
Nominal	2 non-related	2	Fisher's exact test	A study to compare the difference in suicide rates between two ethnic groups
Nominal	1	more than 2	Chi Square test	A study to determine whether or not a group attending a drug detoxification programme is equally divided between a number of different ethnic groups
Nominal	2 non-related	more than 2	Chi Square test	A study to compare the differences in smoking, non-smoking, drinking and non-drinking between males and females
Nominal	more than 2 non-related	more than 2	Chi Square test	A study to compare the differences in smoking, non-smoking, drinking and non-drinking between people in a number of different ethnic groups

Table 5.5

Continued

Level of data	No. of groups	No. of categories	Test	Example of study
Ordinal	1	2	Wilcoxon's signed rank test	A study to determine the average competence level, as measured on a scale, of a group of professionals compared to the known level for whole profession
Ordinal	2 related	2	Wilcoxon's signed rank test	A pre-post, quasi-experimental study to compare the average depression scores, as measured on a scale, of a group of people before and after an intervention to lower depression
Ordinal	2 non-related	2	Mann Whitney U test	A study to compare the average competence levels, as measured on a scale, of two groups of professionals
Ordinal	More than 2 non-related	More than 2	Kruskal Wallis test	A study to compare the differences, as measured on scales of: pain, depression and quality of life, between people in a number of different age groups
Interval/ Ratio	1	2	One sample *t*-test	A study to compare the average blood pressure, as measured on a monitor, of a sub group of people compared to the known average level for a given population
Interval/ Ratio	2 related	2	Dependent means *t*-test	A pre-post quasi-experimental study to compare the average blood pressure, as measured on a monitor, of a group of people before and after intervention to lower blood pressure
Interval/ Ratio	More than 2 non-related	More than 2	One way analysis of variance (ANOVA)	A study to compare the differences in number of units of alcohol consumed, number of cigarettes smoked and average blood pressure between three different age groups of people
Interval/ Ratio	2 non-related	2	Independent means *t*-test	A RCT to compare the mean average number of days spent out of prison per year of a group of high-risk offenders on a mentoring programme compared to a similar group who are not on a mentoring programme
Interval/ Ratio	2 non-related	2	Independent means *t*-test	A double-blind RCT to compare the mean average blood pressure in a group of people taking a blood pressure lowering drug compared to a similar group who are taking a placebo

Statistical significance

As mentioned in previous chapters, it should be remembered that statistical tests do not tell us if our theories and hypotheses are true or correct. They only tell us the likelihood of the results being due to random chance, which allows us to support our hypothesis and reject the null hypothesis. It was mentioned that we do not accept more than a 5% probability of our results being due to chance. This is in effect accepting odds of less than 1 in 20 that you could be wrong. To put this in perspective, you might ask yourself if you would travel on a train knowing that roughly 1 in every 20 trains leaving your station will crash. Alternatively, we could set our significance level lower than that and only accept a less than a 1% probability of being wrong. This is again represented by a 'p' value and written as $p < 0.01$.

It is possible to set our significance level at points in between $p < 0.05$ or $p < 0.01$, for example at $p < 0.03$. However, convention dictates that levels are set at either $p < 0.05$ or $p < 0.01$.

It is worth bearing in mind that at the level of $p < 0.01$ there is still almost a 1% probability (or 1 in 100 chance) that we could be wrong. So let's consider why we might be wrong? How does this happen? Basically, this is normally due to a sampling error – our sample is not representative of the population that we wish to generalise our findings to.

Going back to the example of our experiment to give people with high blood pressure a drug thought to lower it, imagine we did this in the form of a double-blind RCT to compare the mean average blood pressure in a group of people taking a blood pressure lowering drug (intervention group) compared to a similar group who are taking a placebo (control group). We might find at the end of the experiment that in our study group the mean average blood pressure was considerably lower than that of the control group. After doing a t-test, this result was shown to be statistically significant at the level of $p < 0.05$ and you accepted these findings.

Subsequently, we start prescribing this drug for people with high blood pressure but find that it does not seem to work. Several much larger RCTs are then carried out, which demonstrate that the drug has no significant effect compared to placebo. In such a case, we would have made a type 1 error in our original RCT, we rejected the null hypothesis (that the drug has no effect compared to placebo) when we should have accepted it and instead rejected our hypothesis that the drug could lower blood pressure. Remember, there was nearly a 1 in 20 chance that we could be wrong anyway, that our sample may not have been representative of the wider population of people with high blood pressure. Our sample could have, for example, contained a disproportionately high number of people who were susceptible to the placebo effect in the intervention group and a disproportionately high number of people who were not susceptible to the placebo effect in the control group.

Remember, considerable numbers of people can be susceptible to the poorly understood placebo effect, whereby they imagine an inactive substance has had an effect upon them and this power of suggestion actually causes the effect. Indeed, this has been the experience of the author when testing a new painkilling drug, whereby it was observed, after 'unblinding' the data that 40% of people who had painful surgery became pain free after an injection of saline (salt water). (The findings from this study were never published as the drug company who manufactured the drug decided that it worked little better than placebo.) This is not only true of conditions that are experienced subjectively, such as pain and anxiety, but also true of largely physiological conditions. Thus, to recapitulate, a significant number of the intervention group (who actually had the drug but were blinded so did not know it) may have been convinced the drug would lower their blood pressure and it therefore actually did and a significant number of the control group (who had the placebo but were blinded so did not know it) may not have been convinced that whatever they were given would lower their blood pressure and it therefore actually did not. Consequently, the end result would have been lower blood pressures in the study group, when in fact the drug did not really work.

It is also possible to make what is known as a type 2 error, that is when we reject our hypothesis and accept the null hypothesis when in fact we should be rejecting it. There is more chance of making a type 1 error when the significance level is set at $p < 0.05$ and more chance of making a type 2 error when the significance level is set at $p < 0.01$.

This is because with a significance level of p < 0.05 there are almost 5 chances in 100 (or 1 chance in 20) of being wrong, so if 1 train out of every 20 crashes, making a type 1 error is the equivalent of getting on one of those trains that crashes because you thought it would not crash. Conversely, with a significance level of p < 0.01 there is almost a 1 chance in 100 of being wrong, so making a type 2 error is the equivalent of not getting on one of those trains that did not crash, because you thought that it would crash. Thus, with more likelihood of crashing, a type 1 error is easier to make, but with less likelihood of crashing, a type 2 error is easier to make.

The *t*-test

One of the commonly used tests for determining statistical significance is known as the *t*-test, which is suitable for interval and ratio data.

The formula for the *t*-test is as follows:

- Calculate the mean average values for two samples.
- Calculate the standard deviation (SD).
- Calculate the observed difference between both mean values.
- Calculate the standard error (SE) of the mean by dividing the SD by the square root of the number of people in the sample (n).
- Divide the observed difference in mean values by the SE.
- Look up the *t*-value on a table to determine if significant or not and report corresponding p value.

Fortunately computers are now able to do this for us.

Below is a simple example of how to calculate a p value using the *t*-test on a small group of 10 people who had stopped taking morphine for 48 hours and had their mean average systolic blood pressures (BP) during that period compared to their mean systolic BP during a 48 hour period in which they continued to take morphine. This was to assess for raised systolic BP, a known withdrawal symptom occurring on abstinence from morphine.

Mean BP without morphine = 134 (SD 14),
Mean BP with morphine = 133 (SD 14)

$$SE = \frac{SD}{\text{sq root of n (n = 10 people)}} = \frac{14}{3.1} = 4.5$$

$$\text{Observed difference in mean averages} = 134 - 133 = 1$$

$$t = \frac{\text{observed difference in means}}{\text{SE}} = \frac{1}{4.5} = 0.22$$

For a group of 10 people, the cut off point in the statistical table for statistical significance at $p < 0.05$ is 2.262 and for statistical significance at $p < 0.01$ is 3.250, both of which are higher than 0.22, therefore there was no statistically significant change in mean average systolic BP during morphine withdrawal in this group of 10 people, this being contrary to what is generally expected during withdrawal from opioid drugs (Cowan, Wilson-Barnett, Griffiths *et al.* 2005). However, it should be noted that this was a relatively small sample.

Replication

Replication

Sometimes there is no feasible way of discovering if our findings are invalid, that is, if we have made a type 1 or type 2 error, and we can only say at best how confident we can be, based on significance tests on probability samples, that our findings can be generalised to wider populations (Bryman 2004). However, should other researchers wish to replicate our work, whether this is to investigate whether we have made a type 1 or 2 error or to verify our findings for some other reason, we need to demonstrate that this is possible and therefore need to make our methods explicit and replicable.

Systematic review and meta-analysis

Systematic review and meta-analysis

Another common type of analysis of quantitative data is that of the systematic review, as was introduced in Chapter 2 on evidence-based practice. The systematic review represents a form of secondary research and involves a review of all literature identified, appraised and amalgamated to give a summary answer to a question and usually comprises a synthesis of findings from relevant RCTs. The purpose is to find all relevant research and appraise it, based on pre-defined criteria, whereas a narrative review of findings may ignore certain papers that disagree with a particular theory (Bryman 2004). The systematic review is described as a 'scientific' strategy intended to limit bias in the systematic assembly, critical appraisal and synthesis of all of the relevant studies on a particular topic (Omar 2006). A meta-analysis is a particular type of systematic review that employs statistical methods to combine and summarise the results of several studies (Omar 2006). As individual studies may lack statistical power, a meta-analysis can be a useful method for combining results in a meaningful way. This is according to the law of large numbers, whereby evidence that has been tested in a greater number of high quality studies, should load the odds in favour of successful outcomes for the service user (Newman *et al.* 2005).

Number needed to treat

Despite the criticisms of quantitative research presented in the last chapter (and indeed those criticisms highlighted regarding evidence-based practice in Chapter 2), practitioners need to have an idea of what interventions work and how well they work. One of the favoured measures of successful outcome used by meta-analysts is the number needed to treat (NNT). That is, the number of people you would have to treat (or apply an intervention to) in order to achieve a pre-defined successful outcome. In this way data from a large number of studies can be pooled and analysed, in order to calculate a single figure which is a useful indicator of effectiveness. If we use the example of treating pain, and we pre-define our successful outcome as achieving a 50% reduction in pain, it is then possible to calculate NNTs for drugs administered to reduce pain. For example, the NNT for achieving 50% reduction in pain for the commonly purchased drug ibuprofen (Brufen) 400mg is 2.5 (Bandolier 2007). This means that for every five people who take ibuprofen, two of them will experience the desired outcome of 50% pain reduction over 4 to 6 hours, compared with placebo, in pain of moderate to severe intensity.

In order to calculate an NNT for an intervention we need to know how many people had the intervention (the treatment group), how many had it with a successful outcome, how many people had the alternative intervention or placebo (control group) and how many people in the control group experienced a successful outcome. Thus, the calculation is as follows:

- Number who had intervention = 100
- Number who had successful outcome with intervention
  = 75 = 75% (0.75)
- Number who had control = 100
- Number who had successful outcome with control
  = 25 = 25% (0.25)
- Number Needed to Treat = $1/(0.75 - 0.25) = 1/0.50 = 2$

Also, if we focus on an undesired adverse event caused by an intervention – (such as an unpleasant side-effect of a drug) instead of on a successful outcome, it is possible in the same way to calculate the number needed to harm (NNH) for an intervention. Thus, if practitioners have such information on both the effectiveness and safety of interventions they can provide service users with the most appropriate health and social care.

Using the example of pain, we should remember that pain is a subjective experience that does not easily lend itself to quantitative measurement. A commonly used pain measurement tool is a scale that asks the person in pain to score their pain on a scale between 0 and 10, where 0 represents no pain and 10 represents the worst pain imaginable. However, calculating a 50% reduction on a scale of 0–10 is not always possible. Therefore, meta-analysts prefer pain to be scored on a scale of none, mild, moderate, severe and very severe. This is then converted for analysis to a scale of 0–4 whereby none = 0, mild = 1, moderate = 2, severe = 3, very severe = 4. Using such a scale makes it relatively easy to calculate 50% total pain reduction, such as represented by a reduction from 4 to 2 or from 2 to 1.

However, if we think back to our different levels of data, we are converting ordinal categorical data to ordinal numerical data, that is, converting 'moderate' to '2'. While there is no problem in converting 'moderate' to '2', in assuming that 2 is 50% of 4, this is in effect treating the data as ratio, which in fact they are not. This serves to demonstrate that quantitative analysis is not an exact science.

Until recently NNTs and NNHs have been applied largely to treatments or interventions utilised within health care research. However, there is no reason why they cannot be applied to social care.

In fact in some instances NNTs can be more amenable to social work contexts than to health care. For example, we could apply an intervention as part of a youth inclusion programme, intended to reduce criminal offending among youths who are repeat offenders and who spend considerable time in custody. A useful desirable outcome measure might be the amount of time spent outside custody, say one year, among comparable groups of youths, one group having the intervention, another not having it. Thus, time outside custody would constitute ratio data and would be more robust than much of the data that currently informs health care research, such as the use of categorical proxy scales in the important area of pain control.

Interpretation of findings

Interpretation of findings

As Bryman (2004) points out, the researcher usually has to do more than simply rely on their findings and conclusions to inform their own practice; they must convince others of the worthiness of what they have done. Thus, when these findings are published in peer-reviewed publications, they then become part of the stock of knowledge, representing an element of deductivism, as theory has been tested but also an element of inductivism as new or modified theory may emerge (Bryman 2004). However, an important aspect of this process is how the researcher, now in their role as author, interprets their findings. It is tempting to interpret one's own findings in the most appealing way possible. For example, to draw upon an old adage, depending on who we may wish to appeal to, we may describe something as being either 'half full' or 'half empty'.

In the same way, imagine that we were reporting on the findings of a crime survey in an area where burglaries had increased from one a month to two a month. If we were trying to convince our audience of the negative aspects of this we might state that burglaries had doubled, or that they had risen by 100%. Conversely, if we were trying to play these figures down, we might state that there was just one extra burglary a month and that this was nothing to be alarmed about. Thus, we should be wary of reports written by parties with vested interests and remember that authors' conclusions should be appropriate, valid and relevant to the aim of the research and be based on appropriate analysis and interpretation of data.

We should also be on the look out for overstatements, unsubstantiated connections or explanations and results that are inappropriately generalised beyond the scope of the study. Also, we should look out for the author's own views being expressed in the absence of appropriate evidence, for example, in some cases, when it is not possible to identify cause and effect, researchers often interpret this for themselves.

We should also remember, as stated in previous chapters, that all knowledge and therefore evidence is grounded in historical and social circumstances and that cultural or moral values may be translated into 'scientific facts'. Bear in mind that the researcher's values are always likely to be at play in interpreting the findings of studies. (These issues will be returned to in Chapter 9 on critical appraisal of research findings.)

Last, when findings are written up for consumption in the 'public' domain – this can mean both for the 'professional' public and increasingly for the general public, as we see more and more research studies being reported 'second hand' in the mass media, these reports often have a particular sensationalist slant or angle which may not accurately portray the original findings of the study.

While the last two chapters have been concerned with quantitative research methods and analysis of quantitative research data, continuing in the quantitative versus qualitative dichotomy, the following two chapters will focus on qualitative research methods and analysis of qualitative research data.

Chapter 6
Qualitative research methods

Introduction

In the previous two chapters we have looked at some examples of commonly used quantitative research designs, general sampling methods and how quantitative research data can be described, represented, summarised and analysed. However, as was touched upon in Chapter 2, frustration at the inability of quantitative research strategies and approaches to address core concepts and issues of relevance has led to the adoption of alternative research approaches (Parahoo 2006). It should be noted that because some phenomena are not amenable to objective measurement, this does not mean that they cannot be studied by other, subjective methods. Thus, researchers began to realise that in order to fully understand people, we should listen to and observe them, and in this way, we could learn more by interacting with them (Parahoo 2006). Accordingly, more flexible, subjective strategies than in quantitative approaches are now utilised to collect and analyse data, in order to get below the surface of things (Robson 2002, Parahoo 2006).

This chapter will examine a range of qualitative research approaches and will explore some common methods that can be utilised within qualitative approaches, such as: ethnography, phenomenology, discourse analysis and grounded theory. As in the last chapter, which did not detail all types of quantitative research, this chapter will examine only some commonly used types of qualitative research methods.

Research issues in health and social care

What is qualitative research?

Making the distinction between qualitative and quantitative research approaches is not always as straightforward as it might first appear and it may be somewhat simplistic just to view this dichotomy in terms of quantity, objectivity and numbers versus quality, description and subjective meanings (Yates 1998). For example, meanings are also important in the quantitative research approach, as where possible we expect our concepts to have universally shared meaning, as was noted in Chapter 4. Also, quantitative research methods may be open to the subjectivity of the researcher and the study participants, as was noted in the case of developing items for survey questionnaires (Yates 1998).

However, broadly speaking, while quantitative research can be associated with positivism, qualitative research can be associated with a reaction against positivism. In qualitative research, the importance of the subjective experiences of both researcher and participants is emphasised, this being central to the meaning of social life, as well as the importance of social and cultural context in situating different meanings and interpretations. Quantitative research approaches are described as being detached in order to avoid bias, whereas qualitative research approaches are described as facilitating interaction with participants in order to get closer to the topic being investigated, gaining a view of the perceptions, experiences and behaviour of our research participants (Parahoo 2006). In doing so, we use intuition to decide when to continue probing or to stop, or to steer data collection and as we employ the use of 'self' to facilitate responses; the ability to 'read' the situation is important (Parahoo 2006).

DePoy and Gitlin (1994) refer to qualitative research studies as 'naturalistic', as opposed to quantitative studies which they refer to as 'experimental'. However, the problem of how to classify non-experimental quantitative studies then arises. Also, the use of the term 'naturalism' in reference to qualitative research may be confusing in the context of the 'natural' sciences, such as physics or biology and their strong relationship with quantitative research. Robson (2002) chooses to refer to qualitative research as being characterised by 'flexible' research designs and quantitative research as employing 'fixed' designs.

However, despite some variation in terminology, for the purposes of this and other chapters, qualitative research can be seen as a broad, umbrella term comprising a number of diverse and distinct approaches and concepts, including: interpretivism, historicism, relativism and critical realism, both of the latter considered as forms of constructivism. Nonetheless, these approaches and concepts are similar in that they seek to explore and understand human experience, perceptions, motivations, intentions and behaviour (Parahoo 2006).

Qualitative research often takes an interpretive approach to its subject matter; qualitative researchers study things in their natural settings, attempting to make sense of, or interpret, phenomena in terms of the meanings that people bring to them (Denzin & Lincoln 1994). Qualitative research begins by accepting that there is a range of different ways of making sense of the world and is concerned with discovering the meanings seen by those who are being researched and with understanding their view of the world rather than that of the researchers (Jones 1995).

Qualitative research approaches are based on the belief that interpretation is central to the exploration and understanding of social phenomena (Yates 1998, Parahoo 2006). Thus, we find common usage of the term 'interpretivist'. Accordingly, McKenna (1997) observes that while there are similarities and differences between qualitative approaches, they can all be seen as being informed by interpretivist philosophy, thus placing emphasis on subjective interpretation as opposed to objective empirical observations. However, there is also a branch of phenomenology, which could be argued by some purists as being descriptive as opposed to interpretive, but this is something of a philosophical point and is elaborated upon further in the section of this chapter on phenomenology.

McKenna (1997) sees qualitative approaches as being interactive because researchers engage in conversations and with texts, they collect data that reflect participants' perspectives and they analyse these data by taking into account their specific contexts. According to McKenna (1997), in the nursing profession, quantitative research was dominant until the 1970s, when it was realised that certain phenomena, including the core concepts of care that are relevant to practitioners and their clients, require more in-depth understanding. In this way the decision-making processes of the cared for and their carers may be better understood. For example, for service users to be able to participate in decision-making about their own care requires an understanding of their perceptions on the part of service providers (McKenna 1997). While questionnaire surveys may provide measurement scales for phenomena conducive to measurement by such tools, qualitative methods are more appropriate for gaining understanding of people's perceptions and experiences which are less amenable to being measured on a scale.

Terminology box

Interpretivism

- Interpretation is central to the exploration and under-standing of social phenomena.
- While there are differences between qualitative research methods, they are all largely informed by interpretivist philosophy.
- Emphasis is placed on subjective interpretation as opposed to objective observations.

Kuhn (1970) and Feyerabend (1975) challenged the positivist view and stressed the importance of history and previous knowledge in the development of science. McKenna (1997) observes that, as noted in Chapter 3, we are unavoidably influenced by our histories and experiences, our values and beliefs being acquired across time. Thus, because it states that we interpret events and subsequently construct our own realities, this subjective perspective on the world of science may also be referred to as the interpretive-constructivist approach, underpinned by the philosophy of historicism. Furthermore, as noted in Chapters 2 and 3, reality and knowledge of that reality mean different things to different people, therefore reality is a variable concept, being the product of individual reflection, perception and purpose as opposed to being static and objective.

As noted in Chapter 2, Marks (2002) argued that the role of power and ideology in the generation of evidence or facts must not be overlooked and should be carefully analysed. With regard to what Marks (2002) called social constructivist (or relativist) approaches, whatever any individual believes to be the truth, is true for them. Thus, the foundations of knowledge are value laden and contrary to the positive realist approach (returning again to the objective versus subjective dichotomy introduced in Chapter 1), the distinction between objective and subjective is unclear; therefore there is no absolute truth in the social world (Marks 2002).

Marks (2002) argued that critical realism, an alternative approach to the positivist realism that informs quantitative research approaches, views the world as an open system whereby a multiplicity of mechanisms operate simultaneously and affect each other; therefore, the simple positivist view of causation is wrong. Thus, the objective reality of the physical world is not the only valid and useful way of understanding the totality of the experienced universe; the subjective experiences of social, religious, political and cultural beliefs all offer different but equally valid perspectives of the truth and eliminating subjectivity from the truth is impossible (Marks 2002). Marks (2002), echoing Kuhn (1970) and Feyerabend (1975) observed that the same object or event may be interpreted differently by different people, creating a multiplicity of meanings and truths and these are best studied using qualitative research methods.

Likewise, Grypdonck (2006) noted that researchers can only understand perception and behaviour from participants' own perspectives, in their own words and in the context in which they exist, live and work and that while there can be different interpretations of the same phenomena, the purpose of qualitative research is to gain better understanding of how people think and behave as individuals and groups and to acknowledge that health professionals and patients may see the same thing differently.

Similarly, Robson (2002) stated that while there was a need to represent reality, we should acknowledge that such reality will always be from a particular perspective and that phenomena are not independent of the researcher. Thus, holistic exploration of phenomena enables participants to relay the totality of their experience of a particular phenomenon in their terms and not through the lens of researcher-generated variables, which, as already highlighted can be historically, culturally and socially constructed and also interviewer constructed. A flexible (qualitative) approach relies on methods that allow the researcher into the personal, intimate and private world of the participants, using flexible, imaginative, creative and varied strategies, such as interviews, observations, focus groups, analysis of video recordings, letters, diaries and other documents (Robson 2002).

Kuhn (1970) also dismissed the concept of objective truths and argued that as knowledge development was dynamic, there could be no final and permanent truths. Kuhn (1970) argued that due to various paradigm shifts (as noted in Chapter 2), the construction of reality could be seen as an evolutionary and revolutionary process. In this way, new knowledge is continually influenced by previous knowing (Laudan 1977). This approach is attractive to the nursing (and other health and social care professions) because it recognises a pluralistic approach to knowledge development and application. Indeed, problems facing nurses are constantly changing and therefore we must select the theory and the paradigm that are best suited to solving the relevant problem, there seldom being a consistent way of viewing nurses' subjective reality because it is constantly changing, giving rise to new problems (McKenna 1997). Thus, there has been an increasing popularity of qualitative research methods in health and social care, these methods perceived as being more holistic and humanistic, facilitating a more patient/client/service user-centred approach and moving away from traditional, positivist informed research approaches, these, as mentioned in earlier chapters, typically based on the assumptions of the natural sciences (McKenna 1997). This has led to greater emphasis on the uniqueness of the individual's understanding of the world which they inhabit and in particular, understanding of what it is like to experience illness and how people's lives may be changed by it. Accordingly, much value is placed on the views of the recipients of treatment, to enable practitioners to provide appropriate care (McKenna 1997).

Noting that qualitative research methods often utilise an inductive approach, Parahoo (2006) contrasts this to quantitative research methods whereby one knows in advance what variables to study and a deductive approach is often used to test ideas, theories and hypotheses. Conversely, qualitative approaches are used to develop concepts, conceptual frameworks, themes, theories and hypotheses from observations, interviews and interpretation of discourse, conversations and texts, including diaries, letters and historical documents. In utilising an inductive approach, the researcher can remain open to ideas which may emerge from constant reflection on participants and on the researcher's preconceived ideas, listening to or observing people and examining and re-examining one's own perspective, during and after data collection. This is useful when little is known about topics under study or when existing conceptual definitions are inadequate or not adequately reflective of people's experience.

Accordingly, Robson (2002) advocated that a good flexible research design comprises rigorous methods of data collection and analysis, recognition of the possibility of multiple realities, recognition of the researcher as an instrument of data collection and that there also needs to be particular focus on the participant's views. Furthermore, it requires accurate report writing – the researcher must verify the accuracy of findings, data may be analysed in layers and clear writing up of findings should engage and enable the reader to experience what it is like to 'be there', rendering the findings as believable, realistic and accurately portraying the complexities of real life (Robson 2002). This is achieved through the use of interactive, inductive, flexible and reflexive methods of data collection and analysis, the findings presented in a variety of formats including descriptions, themes, conceptual models and theories (Robson 2002, Parahoo 2006).

As stated in Chapter 2, Grypdonck (2006) noted that while quantitative research can prove something has caused an effect, qualitative theory construction can provide deeper understanding of how or why this may be. Thus, qualitative research is important for providing the understanding that is necessary to apply findings from quantitative research properly and to practice safely (Grypdonck 2006). Like McKenna (1997) and Parahoo (2006), Grypdonck (2006) argued that qualitative studies about human behaviour, experience in illness and with regard to meanings in general, remain of great value in judging the desirability of outcomes for success and in contributing to practitioner awareness of the need to contextualise findings, as every patient can be an exception to the rule.

Research issues in health and social care

Qualitative research is important for bringing the perspective of the person to the fore, particularly with regard to the appropriateness of given interventions in cases of chronic illness, enhancing data on the effectiveness of interventions and what it is like to live and cope with long-term illness (Grypdonck 2006). In this way, gaps in understanding between professionals, healthy people and those with chronic conditions can be bridged (Grypdonck 2006). Also, misunderstanding regarding treatment decisions between the prescribers of treatment and patients can be reduced.

Given that some quantitative assessment tools may be unhelpful because they can cause anxiety and may be insensitive, Parahoo (2006) highlights how qualitative research can address the persistent problem of people's non-compliance with health care treatment. Parahoo (2006) believes that qualitative research studies can enlighten us as to why this may happen and which factors can facilitate or hinder treatment and recovery. For example, with regard to how people make decisions about the self-management of chronic conditions, qualitative research has highlighted how people attempt to achieve the balance between living a life whereby they adhere to treatment, which may in itself be debilitating and/or have unpleasant side-effects, or choosing from time to time to violate their therapeutic regime, in this way 'lifting life' above the disease (Grypdonck 2006). Professionals who support people with chronic illness need to be aware of this possibility and qualitative research studies about people living with chronic illness can facilitate such awareness (Grypdonck 2006).

Similarly, we can gain better understanding with regard to exploring and assessing people's knowledge of health and well-being, illness, disease, medication and health services (Parahoo 2006). Also, we may better understand barriers to stopping unhealthy behaviour (and indeed anti-social behaviour), barriers to starting healthy (or socially acceptable) behaviour – such as ensuring good nutrition, the qualities of people who have good outcomes, the nature of resilience in people with chronic conditions, and a general sense and meaning in life among people with various chronic conditions (Parahoo 2006). In addition, qualitative methods can facilitate and enhance user participation in research studies, which is increasingly seen as being ethically sound, particularly among disadvantaged or vulnerable groups.

Commonly used methods

Commonly used methods

Qualitative research often takes place within an evolving design, which may be simultaneously informed by several approaches or traditions of enquiry (Robson 2002). Robson (2002) suggested that within a critical realist framework, theory rather than data is central to explaining reality and that all methods are only capable of producing an approximation of reality, no method being better than the others. Despite this, McKenna (1997) points out that qualitative research methods have their own distinctive procedures. Ethnography focuses on culture, phenomenology focuses on consciousness, discourse analysis focuses on the use of language and grounded theory aims to develop theory through the process of induction (McKenna 1997). However, the overall aim of these methods remains the same, that is, to understand consciousness and culture and the actions and reactions of individuals, groups and organisations, in order to provide access to the worlds of the research participants (McKenna 1997).

Ethnography

Ethnography

Ethnographic research techniques have evolved from the disciplines of social anthropology and sociology. Social anthropological study by researchers from the developed world of largely unknown and undocumented less-developed societies, led to the conclusion that things could not be taken as given – therefore research tools such as rigid questionnaires are often deemed as inappropriate (Yates 1998). Sociology, that is, the study of societies in the developed world by those that live in them, has now incorporated similar techniques, to the point that under the general heading of ethnography, the social anthropology approach is now used in the study of any distinct social, cultural or professional group.

Ethnography, meaning portrait of people, as mentioned, has roots in social anthropology, whereby early anthropologists studied tribal communities and often lived with them, adopting their mannerisms, habits, rituals and customs (Parahoo 2006). The collection of data takes part in the natural environment of those being studied, mediated by the culture in which they live.

Ethnography is based on the premise that behaviour can only be understood if it is studied in the setting in which it occurs. It is recognised that people not only have shared language, but also shared meanings, perceptions, values and norms. The focus is on culture and on gaining a holistic understanding of behaviour and how individuals interact in their respective groups. Ethnographic studies are now broadened beyond tribes and can take place in any number of distinct social settings such as hospitals or prisons, or groups of people, such as gypsies, the police, street gangs, social workers, nurses or hospital patients (Yates 1998). Many television documentaries employ this approach to produce the numerous 'reality' shows that now prevail on our screens.

Robson (2002) recognises ethnography as a well established strategy, whereby the researcher becomes fully immersed in the culture that they are studying, in this way gaining an essential 'insider's' perspective on shared cultural meanings of behaviour, actions, events and contexts. Despite this, even if studying a familiar group, such as an experienced criminology researcher observing police 'canteen culture' Robson (2002) recommends treating each group or situation as if it was anthropologically strange.

While non-participant and participant observation and focus group interviews are common, Robson (2002) notes that no method of data collection is ruled out and that quantitative methods may also be used. In fact, as many sources of data as possible, as long as they are within legal and ethical boundaries, can be drawn upon (Yates 1998). However, direct participant observation across time is commonly utilised and the focus is on the description and interpretation of the culture and social structure of a given social group in which participants are encouraged to voice issues in their own voice and context. This is perceived as the classic method of social anthropology fieldwork (Yates 1998). A holistic approach of inductive, interactional, flexible and creative methods is applied in order to understand the social realities of groups of people, whereby themes gradually emerge during and after the fieldwork.

Robson (2002) also notes some drawbacks of this approach. It can be time consuming. There may be a need for understanding of specialist concepts within socio-cultural systems and the findings are usually written up in a narrative form which may be unfamiliar to those with health or social care backgrounds. Furthermore, there is the danger of the researcher 'going native' – that is, moving from the role of researcher to that of participant and adopting the behaviour and characteristics of those who are being studied. The latter problem was demonstrated during a study into football hooliganism in the 1980s, involving two of the researching journalists who became so embroiled in violent confrontations between opposing groups of football hooligans that they actually started to enjoy it. As Robson (2002) highlights, the ethnographer will often experience the atmosphere, noise, achievements and frustration generated by their participants, particularly in the heat of the moment.

Terminology box

Ethnography
- Ethnography means portrait of people
- Rooted in social anthropology, whereby communities are studied with regard to their mannerisms, habits, rituals and customs
- The task is to document the culture, the perspectives and practices of the people
- The aim is to 'get inside' the way a particular group sees the world.

The type of ethnographic sampling method is usually purposive, as it is necessary to pinpoint and study a particular social group. This does not produce generalisable results but is intended to produce a specific and rich understanding of a particular group, so it is therefore necessary to select a useful group, which may require a considerable amount of time, even before the study begins (Yates 1998). Given the diversity of data collection methods, it is possible to end up with a large body of text, including documents, field notes and audio and video recordings, which is known as a 'corpus'. There is no well defined consensus on how to analyse data from ethnographic studies and in each unique situation it is common for the researcher to use their personal experience to make sense of the findings (Yates 1998). Furthermore, it is suggested that there has been a neglect of the use of ethnography in research due to no standard interpretation of what ethnography is and confusion over the possibility of ethnography being perceived as both a process and a product (Savage 2000).

Phenomenology

Phenomen-ology

As indicated earlier in this chapter, McKenna (1997) noted that there has been an increasing realisation that knowledge and knowing should not only be dependent on facts, objective data and understanding people by reducing them to numbers. While such positivism was appropriate for application to the natural sciences, this was an erroneous way of viewing knowledge development in the social sciences (McKenna 1997). McKenna (1997) notes further that understanding the meaning of phenomena to particular individuals – the way things appear to people – requires the use of reflection and that meaning and perception can be better than detached quantification.

Similarly, the German philosopher Husserl (1962) observed that positivism was not capable of dealing with human experience because it only deals with observable entities and objective reality. Thus, the best way to discover truth is to consider the essence of things – in particular what meaning the human mind has for that thing. Hence, phenomenology, as developed by Husserl (1962), is a research approach informed by the interpretivist philosophical tradition, with the purpose of investigating consciousness as conceived and experienced by those being studied (Parahoo 2006).

The emphasis of phenomenology is on individuals as opposed to emphasis on groups and social structures as in ethnography. Focus is on the individual's interpretation of lived experiences and how they express them, with an emphasis on describing how they experience particular phenomena, thus, the name phenomenology. This approach is based on the notion that only those who experience phenomena are capable of communicating them and that the researcher's empirical observations are limited in understanding the perceptions of individuals. Husserl (1962) proposed the concept of bracketing, which means that the researcher needs to 'bracket' or suspend their preconceptions, so that these do not interfere with the respondent's description of their experience. This then can also be described as descriptive phenomenology. Given Robson's (2002) observation that reality and associated phenomena will not be independent of the researcher, this would seem reasonable. However, Robson (2002) also stated that we should acknowledge that reality will always be from a particular perspective and that phenomena are not independent of the researcher. Thus, it can be argued that in undertaking descriptive phenomenology, it is impossible to avoid one's own interpretation of phenomena.

Accordingly, an alternative within phenomenology, the hermeneutical approach seeks to discover exactly how respondents came to experience phenomena in the particular way that they do. (The term comes from hermeneutics – the process of examination of religious texts and finding the correct interpretation from several different ones and which is now applied to any texts and also to conversations, and this approach was developed by one of Husserl's students, Heidegger (1962).) Heidegger (1962) believed that in order to properly understand respondents' experiences it is necessary to reject bracketing because we cannot separate the respondent's descriptions from our own interpretations, preconceptions and prejudices, as these are regarded as essential in understanding how people experience phenomena differently.

Furthermore, Heidegger (1962) did not believe that mere description of experience was enough, that we need to know about people's personal history, education, social class and psychological make-up, because all of these can influence the ways in which individuals experience phenomena. Thus, there is a 'fusion of horizons' when the preconceptions of the researcher meet with those who are studied (Wilde 1992). In this way, focusing on individuals' backgrounds and social and historical conditioning is seen as useful in determining how an individual interprets the world in a given context.

Another variant of phenomenology, that of critical science, stresses that meanings can be open to criticism McKenna (1997).

According to Powers and Knapp (1995) critical theory assumes that people are dominated by social conditions, including ideologies that oppress and constrain. As Marks (2002) warned, the role of power and ideology in the generation of evidence or facts must not be overlooked. Thus, critical theory assumes that all research and underlying theory are socio-political constructions and that human societies are by their very nature oppressive (Powers & Knapp 1995). However, when people become enlightened (as they did during the 'Enlightenment' discussed in Chapter 1), this renders all interpretations of the world open to criticism. Within such enlightenment, the importance of social transformation through education is emphasised, to facilitate knowledge and a sense of 'self' in relation to the world, whereby people have reflective clarity, self-determination, empowerment, emancipation, the ability to critique and subsequently to effect change, as in the example of feminism (Powers & Knapp 1995).

Despite these different schools of phenomenology, the basis of phenomenology is the notion that the essence of people's existence is the experience and meanings they perceive within the world in which they live (McKenna 1997). Thus, as mentioned earlier, in this context the perceived world is the real world.

Terminology box

Phenomenology
- Embraces subjectivity
- Denotes an essential relationship between conscious subjects and their objects
- Objects cannot be adequately described in isolation from the subject
- Focus is on the individual's interpretation of lived experiences and how they express them, with an emphasis on describing how they experience particular phenomena.

Discourse analysis

Discourse
analysis

While the term 'discourse' may represent a system of knowledge, as in 'a discourse of physics', in qualitative research, discourse analysis represents a particular approach to dealing with data, whereby language and communication are seen as social activities that have structures which need to be explored (Yates 1998). According to Parahoo (2006), discourse analysis is relatively new in health care research. It is based on the theory that language and communication are not neutral and passive mediums which merely convey a message, but they in fact play an active role in constructing our identities and social relationships (Parahoo 2006). Indeed, how we express ourselves is not a neutral act, what we say, the tone, the timing, are full of values, meanings and intentions (Parahoo 2006). We need to examine these closely in order to increase our understanding of human behaviour, in particular how, through language and interaction, we shape and in turn are shaped by our world (Parahoo 2006). Furthermore, as with data collection within ethnographic and phenomenological approaches, what is spoken and written should be analysed in a social, political and historical context.

Terminology box

Discourse analysis
- Analysis of communication and language systems both verbal and written, based on theory that they are not neutral, passive mediums
- The tone and timing of what we communicate are full of values, meanings and intentions
- We need to uncover these to increase our understanding of human behaviour.

Discourse analysis may be seen as either a competing or complementary approach to dealing with textual data. Main sources of data are conversations between participant and interviewer, written documents, case notes and letters (Yates 1998). Foucault (1972) was influential in the development and direction of discourse analysis as a way of providing critical frameworks with the purpose of unmasking power relationships. For example, it is possible to acquire or lose power through the use of language, such as in negotiations regarding decision-making between carers and those that they care for.

While discourse analysis represents a specific type of qualitative data analysis, conversely, this derives from a philosophical position influenced by positivism (Yates 1998). Indeed, discourse analysis is reliant on ideas derived from the discipline of linguistics, which is informed by positivist assumptions that language can be broken down and studied using the same methods as natural science. However, it has also been suggested that what actually constitutes discourse analysis as a research practice is still unclear (Yates 1998).

Grounded theory

Grounded theory

Robson (2002) observes that grounded theory is a more recently developed research approach intended to develop theory with regard to a particular situation, where theory is derived from the study itself. This is now utilised in many professional settings and has become popular in health-related ones. McKenna (1997) notes that as yet another alternative to the hypothetico-deductive approach of positivism, Glaser and Strauss (1967) developed an inductive approach to research, whereby hypotheses and theories emerge out of, or are 'grounded' in data. Thus, grounded theory is not in itself a distinct theory but a description of how theories are developed. In this way, grounded theories can be inductively derived or discovered from the study of representative phenomena, then developed and provisionally verified through further data collection and analysis. In this way it is possible to begin with a given area of study from which a relevant theory emerges, which can then, if necessary, be tested deductively through quantitative research.

Strauss (1987) describes grounded theory as being based on a 'concept-indicator model' which directs the conceptual coding of a set of empirical indicators, the latter indicators are actual data – behavioural actions and events, observed or described in documents and in the words of interviewees and informants. According to Strauss (1987) there may be many indicators (such as actions and events) which are examined and then coded, identifying them as indicators of a class of actions, events or behaviours and then assigning this class a name, thereby categorising it. In this way, we are 'forced' into confronting similarities and differences and degrees of consistency of meaning among indicators, generating uniformity (which becomes a conceptual category) and then other indicators are compared to the category, enabling refinement of and 'best fit' to data. Further properties of conceptual categories are then generated until codes are verified and 'saturated', saturation implying that further data collection will not modify existing categories or generate new ones. This is known as the constant comparison method, that is, the repeated comparison of

Terminology box

Grounded theory
- Research approach intended to develop theory, whereby theory is derived from the study
- Through a series of carefully planned steps, develops theoretical ideas
- Theory must arise from collected data and not external sources
- Process of inductive theory development, based on observation.

information from data collection and emerging theory (Strauss 1987). However, Strauss (1987) warns of the complexity of capturing reality and making convincing sense of it.

Robson (2002) questions whether it is possible to start a research study without having any pre-existing theoretical ideas or assumptions and sees tensions between the evolving and inductive nature of flexible study design and the more systematic approach of grounded theory. Furthermore, according to Robson (2002) it may be difficult to decide when categories are saturated or when theory is sufficiently developed. Also particular types of prescribed categories as components of theory may not be appropriate for a given study. In addition, Bryman (2004) noted that Glaser felt that Strauss was too prescriptive and over-emphasised the development of concepts at the expense of developing theories. Lastly, as with discourse analysis, there is considerable controversy about what a grounded theory approach actually entails, therefore, what actually constitutes grounded theory as a research practice remains unclear (Yates 1998).

Criticisms of qualitative research approaches

Criticisms of qualitative research

Various commentators have raised criticisms about qualitative research and data analyis. Strauss (1987) states that, compared to quantitative methods, qualitative analysis methods are rudimentary and there is a need for effective theory, without which, grounding in data will be speculative and therefore ineffective. Parahoo (2006) warns of findings being perceived as unscientific, not generalisable, subjective and journalistic. However, Parahoo (2006) highlights the important difference between anecdotes that are without critical evaluation and explicit sampling, systematic, rigorous data collection and analysis. Parahoo (2006) also notes that findings may not be seen as valid or reliable because the researchers are too involved and therefore not objective or consistent. Furthermore, findings are not replicable, yet qualitative researchers do not see this as a weakness; they maintain that it is important not to remain detached, otherwise we cannot obtain an in-depth understanding of phenomena.

Also, there is the problem of relying on self-report from respondents, in that it is questionable whether their answers are reliable. However, the same can be said of quantitative approaches; it could be asked whether a quantitative question-naire will reliably elicit truthful responses. On the other hand, it could be argued that there may be less chance of a respondent telling the truth if they are questioned in an intimate face to face interview as opposed to completing an anonymous questionnaire.

Parahoo (2006) argues that hand-picked, localised samples are unrepresentative and although most studies can be of value beyond the sample studied, the findings are largely non-generalisable. However, while case studies may strictly only be applicable to a particular case, it is fair to say generalisations can be made from and about cases and that whole fields of knowledge about ethics, law and psychology may be constructed from case study generalisations.

There are also limitations in that there is a problem of deciding which interpretation of findings is more valid than another, as conflicting interpretations may cause problems. One way of achieving this is for perceived experts in a given field to validate study findings. Sandelowski (1993) maintains though that no matter how experienced experts may be, it is questionable as to whether they are in any position to validate the findings of studies in which they played no part. Robson (2002) warns that in interpreting findings we need to be careful of imposing a framework on what is happening, as opposed to letting this emerge, and it is necessary to trace the route by which you came to your own interpretation. There is also the danger of not considering competing theories seriously enough and having prolonged involvement in a study which may increase the threat of researcher bias (Robson 2002). Furthermore, Robson (2002) argues that despite much debate, the concepts of validity and reliability are often avoided by proponents of qualitative research design and that validity is more to do with exercises such as checking the accuracy of tape interviews, as opposed to demonstrating validity through testing.

Robson (2002) advocates the use, where possible, of triangulation to demonstrate validity, this may be in the form of observer, method, theory or data triangulation. (The concept of triangulation will be returned to in Chapter 8.) Other useful techniques for demonstrating reliability are enlisting peer advice and/or support, having study respondents checking through data, leaving an audit trail of raw data, such as transcripts of original interviews, avoiding common pitfalls such as equipment failure and environmental interferences and searching for cases which challenge one's own theory.

McKenna (1997) believes that in qualitative research there is risk of method slurring, whereby seeking views and attitudes based on lived experience may not necessarily constitute phenomenology and that studying individuals in their own setting or environment does not always constitute ethnography, as all approaches seek to study people's experiences and perceptions in the context of their natural environment, which makes it difficult to differentiate between approaches. With regard to coding in general, Bryman (2004) warns that in coding we may actually lose context, effect fragmentation of data and in doing so lose the thread of the narrative; also we can end up with too many codes. In addition, it may be argued that grounded theorising involves such a rigorous research process that this may be likened to positivism, as opposed to idealism, relativism or interpretivism (Yates 1998). However, despite the above criticisms, Robson (2002) suggests that merely by working (or claiming to be working) within a particular tradition it is possible to get shelter from criticism.

Discussion

According to Grypdonck (2006), qualitative health researchers still have to position themselves in a world that is dominated by the 'ideology' of evidence-based health care practice. Grypdonck (2006) states that qualitative researchers feel they should have a higher place in the hierarchy of research generated evidence, because consensus, opinion and qualitative research are still perceived by many to be at the very low end. While sometimes qualitative research is distinguished from the other two, sometimes it is not. Thus, invariably qualitative research is perceived as the lowest form of research which is to be provisionally used, pending the generation of better evidence (Leys 2003). Grypdonck (2006) also believes that because qualitative research still does not enjoy the same recognition from funders as quantitative research, unless in mixed method designs (these will be discussed in Chapter 8), there is still more emphasis on the funding of studies which involve outcome and intervention based research. Grypdonck (2006) advises that while evidence-based health care practice is here to stay, qualitative researchers must not let their research become undermined and to be aware of the 'gatekeeping' effect quantitative researchers have with regard to publishing qualitative papers in high impact journals. Grypdonck (2006) observes that in reaction to this, qualitative researchers have been attempting to demonstrate the trustworthiness of qualitative findings as expressed in criteria that quantitative researchers can understand and use, such as the meta-synthesis of findings, this being parallel to quantitative meta-analysis. In addition, as mentioned above, in the same way that analysis of grounded theory data studies has been likened to positivism (Yates 1998), Grypdonck (2006) also suggests that techniques of coding and analysis have been adapted from quantitative research methods.

Despite Grypdonck's (2006) reservations, Robson (2002) perceived a trend in the increasing use of qualitative data collection in social research, to the extent that it is seen by some as being privileged in comparison to quantitative research, although Robson (2002) noted that certain 'outposts' such as that of medicine were still orientated towards quantitative research approaches. However, even the latter field has been changing in recent years and it is now increasingly recognised that qualitative inquiry can improve the description and explanation of complex, real-world phenomena pertinent to health services research (Bradley *et al.* 2007).

Robson (2002) believes that designs based largely on flexible methods which generate qualitative data are perceived as respectable and acceptable in social research, including that relating to health and social care. It should be remembered that clinical expertise is the integration of scientific findings, reflected experience, observations, and knowledge, synthesised across time and continually adapted to reflect new information and experiences. Qualitative research contributes to this, as each piece of information, wherever it comes from, is compared to existing information, interpreted and accorded a status, possibly only a provisional one. Although the scientific approach is largely associated with quantitative research, other approaches are not less scientific because they do not explain phenomena in prescribed positivist terms. Alternative approaches to quantitative research recognise that humans may think and act rationally but that this may not happen all of the time, in every circumstance and in a mechanical way. Humans have feelings, emotions, motivations, beliefs, customs and environmental influences which are not necessarily captured by quantitative approaches, which emphasise objectivity and precise measurement.

Conclusion

Grypdonck (2006) acknowledges that findings from experiments can be impressive and potent but may mean nothing if not complemented by other types of knowledge such as that generated by qualitative research. Experiments and surveys have limitations and we need methods informed by positions other than positivism. Qualitative methods inform us about the rich texture of everyday social life, with a focus on meanings as opposed to attempting to measure social life (Grypdonck 2006). Qualitative analysis and discourse analysis can be seen as ways of researching the meanings embedded in the actions and products of individuals and societies. These methods developed out of criticisms of the limitations of quantitative research, and represent a shift from measuring to understanding (Grypdonck 2006).

Strauss (1987) maintains that because social phenomena are complex, there is a need for conceptually dense theory accounting for variations in phenomena studied, and that there are no hard and fast rules given the diversity of settings. Therefore it is possible to have general guides, which because of their general nature may be useful to a broad spectrum of disciplines regardless of tradition or theoretical approach. Strauss (1987) likens qualitative inquiry to intensive microscopic examination which can bring out amazing complexities, and facilitate successfully evolving complex interpretations.

Interpretation of a situation is not always easy using only quantitative approaches, as there is often a need not only to understand meanings but also to create them (Grypdonck 2006). Robson (2002) believes that inductive, interactional and holistic goals are best achieved by flexible, creative and penetrative methods. This flexibility is well demonstrated by the fact that, while quantitative data collection methods must be decided in advance, qualitative data collection methods can be adapted, to 'get closer' to who or what is being studied, and require no fixed sample size (Grypdonck 2006). In this way the researcher can decide to interview more people and can hand pick them, and can decide to stop when it is decided that the point of 'saturation' has been reached (Grypdonck 2006).

To care for people and promote change of behaviour needs in-depth understanding of concepts such as experience, belief, motivation and intention and quantitative research can only partly address this need (McKenna 1997). An in-depth understanding of people's thinking and behaviour is required to understand issues that are of direct relevance to practitioners and policy-makers in health and social care. Doing so requires the adoption of some of the main qualitative approaches described in this chapter: ethnography, phenomenology, discourse analysis and grounded theory. However, it should be borne in mind that there is not complete agreement over what constitutes certain qualitative approaches, such as grounded theory and discourse analysis and that there is still debate about the finer differences between description and interpretation.

Continuing with qualitative research, the next chapter discusses analysis of qualitative research data.

Chapter 7
Analysis of qualitative data

Introduction: what comprises qualitative data?

As with making a distinction between qualitative and quantitative research approaches, to state that qualitative data are those which are not quantitative would be too simplistic a dichotomy. However, in view of the descriptions of qualitative research methods in previous chapters, it can be said that qualitative data are those which hold meanings, which are richer than quantitative data, given that the latter are derived from measures and numbers, often collected in deliberately constructed, artificial situations. For example, quantitative data may come from experiments that employed a highly controlled or closed system, thereby excluding aspects of the real world, or from surveys that impose the researcher's theories and models, and only allow limited responses to complex questions, which may serve to distort the truth about complex behaviour.

In contrast, qualitative data may comprise a more extensive range of material, allowing deeper, richer insights into the finer detail of people, social contexts and practices. This material can include texts, sounds, pictures, film, poetry, books, transcripts of conversations, letters and other cultural and social artefacts. So, while it is apparent that numbers, quantities and measurements permeate our everyday life, these concepts are not very well-suited to assessing variables and meanings such as happiness, sadness, anger, sympathy, boredom, excitement, desire or interest.

Despite this, as noted in Chapter 4, attempts are made to find the best indicators or proxy measures for those concepts which are not directly measurable. Consequently, there are scales available for the quantitative measurement of, for example, intelligence, such as the intelligence quotient scale and there are numerous quality of life scales that are used in health and social care practice and research. However, these scales do not necessarily capture the true workings of the human mind nor do they capture the true quality of physical, social or psychological aspects of life, such as, for example, what it really means and is like to be 'addicted' to a drug. Indeed, as was highlighted in Chapter 3 on defining our terms when developing a research question, do we really know what addiction actually means? However, it is through qualitative research that we may collect and analyse data to help inform the answers to such questions and thus become ever more enlightened.

Analysing qualitative data

Analysing qualitative data

It should be noted that with regard to quantitative research, the analysis of data starts once all data have been collected. Furthermore, quantitative data are perceived as objective because data analysis is replicable through the same statistical tests, or, they may be challenged by applying different tests to the same results. Conversely, once again bearing in mind the qualitative versus quantitative dichotomy, qualitative data are largely subjective. Furthermore, in qualitative studies, analysis takes place as data are collected, so, as the researcher undertakes further collection, it is necessary to remember and reflect upon what has already been collected. Once all the data are collected, a further systematic analysis will then take place (Parahoo 2006). For example, analysis of data derived from ethnographic studies follows a pattern, whereby data collection can overlap with coding. Thus, an idea is formulated, data are collected, coding, data analysis and interpretation take place, more data are collected, coded, analysed and interpreted and so on, until there is a final and conclusive interpretation. Parahoo (2006) notes that data are recorded in a number of ways, such as field notes, audio and video recordings, memos, diaries, letters, leaflets, case notes, all considered as 'texts' for analysis in order to unravel and make sense of phenomena.

Analysis of qualitative data

It is suggested that there are no absolute rules governing the analysis of qualitative data, although there are some general approaches (Bryman 2004), and a number of traditions (Yates 1998). As noted in the last chapter in the section on grounded theory, Bryman (2004) states that when starting with a large corpus of unstructured material, coding is the key process whereby theory is derived from data, the data being systematically gathered and analysed in tandem, repeatedly referring back to previous texts. According to Bryman (2004) open coding is the process of breaking down, examining, comparing, conceptualising and categorising data, in this way yielding concepts that can then be grouped and categorised. Axial coding is the process of putting data back together in new ways by making connections between categories, linking codes to contexts, consequences, patterns of interaction and possible causes. Selective coding, as the name suggests, involves selecting the core category, relating it to others and validating relationships, the core category acting as the 'storyline' that frames the account of whatever has been studied (Bryman 2004). Bryman (2004) also describes the process of moving from codes that are close to data, which can be classified as detailed, to more selective, classified as common, abstract concepts or phenomena of interest. Also, new codes may be generated by combining initial codes.

Bryman (2004) describes 'concepts' as the labels assigned to discrete phenomena, these being the building blocks of theory. 'Categories' are concepts that have been elaborated upon with regard to representation of real-world phenomena, these being at a higher level of abstraction than concepts. Subsequently a category may then become a core category around which other categories pivot (Bryman 2004). Furthermore, it should be remembered that in coding texts, it is possible to code the same section of text in different ways; categories may then be based on relationships between codes, which could provide a meaningful description or a complex theory about something (Yates 1998). Qualitative analysis also allows for the probing and clarification of contradictions and inconsistencies, in particular, when more than one contact with participants occurs and when several data sources are analysed, such as in grounded theory and ethnography.

Bryman (2004) also highlights the idea of narrative analysis, which emphasises the stories that people tell in the course of interviews, and has become a distinctive strategy for qualitative data analysis. These stories arise both from questions designed to elicit them, whereby the interviewer may be implicated in story construction, and also from questions that are not designed to elicit a particular story. This is also known as a biographical or life history approach, or biographical narrative (Bryman 2004).

With regard to the terminology applied to qualitative data analysis, Parahoo (2006) observes that the terms 'codes', 'themes' and 'categories' are sometimes used interchangeably. However, Weber (1983) defines a category as a group of words with similar meanings, and a theme as a cluster of words with different meanings or connotations that together refer to a theme or issue. Arride-Stirling (2001) defines basic themes as simple characteristics of data, which on their own say very little and need to be seen in the context of other basic themes, which together represent organising themes. Middle order themes organise basic themes into clusters of similarity, which are more revealing and global themes are sets of organising themes, which provide the context of a given analysis.

In addition to the general framework for analysing grounded theory data as described in the previous chapter (Glaser & Strauss 1967), Parahoo (2006) highlights other specific frameworks for analysing qualitative data, including those proposed by Stern (1980) and Strauss and Corbin (1998) for grounded theory data, and those proposed by Van Kamm (1966), and Strauss and Corbin (1998) for phenomenological data. One of the more commonly used frameworks for analysing phenomenological data is that proposed by Colaizzi (1978) which is divided into seven stages:

1. Transcripts are read to elicit an overall view and feeling.
2. Significant statements are extracted.
3. Formulated meanings are extracted from statements.
4. Formulated meanings are clustered into themes – extraction of main themes.
5. Results are integrated into an exhaustive description of the phenomenon.
6. Findings are validated through participants.
7. Parts are re-synthesised/reconstituted to present a new understanding of the phenomenon.

Analysis of qualitative data

More recently, computer assisted qualitative data software (CAQDAS) has become available that can manage large amounts of data and can be used for indexing, coding, storing, retrieval and organisation of data and theory testing. Parahoo (2006) notes further that although researchers have initially been slow to start using computer analysis packages such as ETHNOGRAPH, QSR NUD*IST and NVIVO, despite their availability for over a decade, now there is a noticeable increase in the use of these programs. However, Parahoo (2006) warns that computer analysis may lead to a rigid and unreflexive approach, lacking creativity and perception and suggests that in small scale studies the manual approach is still recommended.

Thus, the basic principles of qualitative analysis and data management involve: indexing, summarising and transcription techniques. Generally, a thematic approach to data analysis is taken, involving the basic activities of coding, categorising and identifying themes and emerging theory. Parahoo (2006) states that we need to open up and break down data into as many parts or categories as can be identified and then group these into manageable themes. The levels of this process are not distinct or linear, and it begins during data collection, with researchers continually moving forward and backward between levels or stages, continually re-visiting them, until a comprehensive understanding of the phenomenon as a whole is ready to be reported.

Also, when contemplating qualitative data, it should be remembered that tone, hesitation and repetition in participants' responses and the presence of others are all relevant to the researcher who is trying to make sense of what is being said and the context in which it is said and even periods of silence have meaning. Furthermore, qualitative data analysis often involves re-reading and re-visiting concepts and categories in the same way that when we watch a film for the second or third time we might see something that we did not notice the first time or we may perceive something differently to the first time. We also make use of personal experience to make sense of qualitative data, which contrasts with the quantitative approach of using specific mathematical, statistical testing, the choice of which is usually determined by the level of data collected and the type of study.

Therefore it could be said that data are not merely 'out there' waiting to be collected, but that data can be selected and shaped in certain ways (Yates 1998). The following chapter discusses the possibility of combining qualitative and quantitative research approaches.

Chapter 8
Combining quantitative and qualitative research approaches

Introduction

As was noted in earlier chapters, making the distinction between qualitative and quantitative research approaches is not always as straightforward as it might first appear. Furthermore, it was suggested that while quantitative research can demonstrate an effect, qualitative research can provide deeper understanding of how or why this may be. Thus, qualitative research can be important in providing the understanding necessary to apply the findings from quantitative research properly and safely to practice (Grypdonck 2006). While it is suggested that we cannot feasibly use the philosophical assumptions, rules and norms from one research paradigm to evaluate the process and outcomes of another, clearly there is more than one way to research human beings (Smith 1998). So, while it may be reasonable to suggest that qualitative and quantitative approaches complement each other, could it be feasible to combine them? In the complex and rapidly changing society (and world) that we inhabit, the process of research does not exist in a vacuum. Thus, we may need to innovate with existing theoretical assumptions and methods and subsequently we may decide that certain fundamentals need to be rethought (Smith 1998). We may ask ourselves if it is possible for researchers to bridge the gap between attempts to develop general explanations that hold good across a range of similar situations (quantitative) and attempts to understand the complexity of a particular situation (qualitative), as both approaches elicit useful and interesting information (Smith 1998).

Combining approaches

Combining approaches

Using the example of the nursing profession, some 10 years ago the idea of combining quantitative and qualitative research approaches was still being described as controversial and it was warned that few guidelines were in existence for carrying this out (Shih 1998). However, Shih (1998) had noted the growing emphasis on combining qualitative and quantitative methods in a single study, this practice often referred to as 'triangulation'. Closs and Cheater (1999) suggested that, in the context of perceived 'paradigmatic entrenchment' with regard to resistance to the introduction of EBP, the qualitative versus quantitative debate was becoming increasingly anachronistic and irrelevant. Indeed, more recently Kinn and Curzio (2005) have noted that there are a growing number of authors who argue the case for integrating qualitative and quantitative methods. Despite the two approaches being designed to answer different types of questions, the two have been combined for a number of reasons, including meeting different needs at different stages of a project, compensating for shortcomings in a particular method and for the purposes of triangulation (Kinn & Curzio 2005).

Terminology box

Triangulation

Triangulation is a term originally used in surveying and navigation to plot the location of a third point through using two known points. It was first used as a metaphor in social science during the 1950s for the use of multiple methods to describe a single construct (Shih 1998). More recently, triangulation in research has been broadly defined as the combination of two or more theories, data sources, methods or investigators in one study of a single phenomenon (Denzin 1989).

Noting that qualitative and quantitative research traditions were derived from different philosophical paradigms and are by no means interchangeable, Shih (1998) suggested that both could be valuable as long as they met the obligation of fulfilling their prescriptive investigative norms, as far as their respective disciplines were concerned. Shih (1998) predicted that in using triangulation, the deficiencies intrinsic to a single-investigator, single-site, single-theory, single-method or single unit of analysis will possibly be overcome.

Kinn and Curzio (2005) observed that combining different methods is perceived as increasingly important as researchers and practitioners recognise that RCTs and other quantitative methods are unable to answer all of the questions that are relevant to the evaluation and assessment of increasingly complex health care interventions and systems. There has been an increasing emphasis based upon the value of research, specifically the need for members of all clinical professions (and social care professions) to be capable of undertaking research and to be able to apply the findings to practice, particularly evidence-based practice. This, as mentioned in Chapter 2 has promoted the quantitative method of the RCT to 'gold standard' status in providing good quality evidence (Kinn & Curzio 2005). However, as has also been mentioned in earlier chapters, RCTs have their weaknesess, for example, a number of health (and social care) interventions do not readily lend themselves to investigation by RCT and some such experiments would be unethical (Kinn & Curzio 2005). For example, it would not be ethical to give a placebo drug to people who are dying from terminal illness if there were alternatives that may work. However, as discussed in earlier chapters, Kinn and Curzio (2005) suggest the RCT can benefit from being utilised in tandem with qualitative approaches in order to obtain the views of both practitioners and service users so that evidence is put into practice appropriately.

Kinn and Curzio (2005) observed that historically, nursing research has not always been related to practice, possibly because the qualitative/quantitative divide has led to the proponents of different approaches falling into different camps. However, as more research is undertaken in order to widen the evidence base for care delivery, there is a need for a more flexible approach (not to be confused with Robson's (2002) definition of flexible studies being synonymous with qualitative research), which is likely to require the use of a variety of different research methods, sometimes in combination (Kinn & Curzio 2005).

Research issues in health and social care

In undertaking a review of combining qualitative and quantitative research methods in health care, Kinn and Curzio (2005) found that in some cases quantitative research had been the major approach. Also, they noted that mixing methods was not always appropriate and that some studies appeared to be weaker than they might otherwise have been had a single method been used. They suggest that while it is clear that the rigour of each method must be assessed separately before combining them and that resolving conflicting demands of different methods is essential, there is no single, accepted way of assessing the quality of studies that combine qualitative and quantitative research. In using two sets of questions to appraise the reviewed papers it was apparent that not all of the criteria used were applicable to each study and could potentially cause conflict and contradiction, as issues that may be appropriate for one method may not be for another (Kinn & Curzio 2005). Also, it should be borne in mind that the ontological and epistemological assumptions from different qualitative methods have an impact on the way results may be integrated (Kinn & Curzio 2005).

Kinn and Curzio (2005) recommended that when findings within a combined study are contradictory, there needs to be a coherent discussion of the results otherwise this could lead to publication bias, as generally, studies that appear to have contradictory findings do not get published. In the papers that they appraised, Kinn and Curzio (2005) were able to identify the potential for integration of methods relative to the subject area, although this was not always made explicit by the authors of these papers. In some studies, where the results were properly integrated by the authors it was observed that the outcomes from the research were more convincing than they might otherwise have been.

Kinn and Curzio (2005) predicted that in the future, when researching interventions comprising direct care, there will be an increasing requirement to examine interactions between service users and professionals, practitioner knowledge, communication skills and attitudes. This will become ever more important as service users become more knowledgeable, for example through acquiring knowledge from the internet (Kinn & Curzio 2005).

The tradition of having a narrow, single method focus will be challenged and those with understanding of the strengths and weaknesses of different approaches will need to ensure that appropriate techniques are applied to effectively answer increasingly complex research questions. However, despite the increasing prominence of mixed method approaches, Kinn and Curzio (2005) remind us that single method approaches will still be important.

Kinn and Curzio (2005) concluded that while an increasing number of papers purporting to report the findings of combined method research are being published, the debate around integrating qualitative and quantitative research is continuing. However, further work is required to refine and develop ways of combining methods in order to allow the full potential of integration to be realised. This will include the use of computer programs that will be able to provide added value to using large data sets, bringing together mixed groups of qualitative and quantitative researchers who can contribute their expertise within research teams, as well as changes within education to reflect in undergraduate and post-graduate curricula the debate around this subject (Kinn & Curzio 2005).

In discussing the value of combining qualitative and quantitative research approaches, Foss and Ellefsen (2002) argue that triangulation is justified, given the complexity of health services, the understanding of which requires the use of multiple methods and perspectives. Acknowledging that different kinds of knowledge are gained through different methods, Foss and Ellefsen (2002) state that the epistemology of triangulation should not be seen as a mixture of two different epistemological positions, rather as an epistemological position in its own right. They also argue that triangulation should not be seen as an abandonment of one's own view but rather an extension of it. Observing that the quantitative research approach in the field of health services has been criticised for not taking personal experiences of illness into account and that some qualitative research has been accused of romanticism, Foss and Ellefsen (2002) suggest that method triangulation has the potential to prevent such tendencies by producing knowledge that is placed in different positions according to its closeness to human experiences. Noting the epistemological diversity and complexity of health care practice, Foss and Ellefsen (2002) conclude that findings originating from different methods can represent worthwhile challenges to each other and that this process provides a richer and perhaps more authentic description of issues under investigation.

In noting that quantitative and qualitative approaches can be used to study the same phenomena and facilitate concept refinement and development, Parahoo (2006) presents six types of method triangulation as proposed by Kimchi *et al.* (1991). These are as follows:

- Theory – an assessment of the utility and power of competing theories in hypotheses
- Data – the use of multiple data sources with similar foci to obtain diverse views about a topic, for the purpose of validation
- Investigator – the use of two or more 'research trained' investigators with divergent backgrounds to explore the same phenomenon
- Analysis – the use of two or more approaches to the analysis of the same set of data
- Methods – the use of two or more research methods in one study
- Multiple – the use of more than one type of triangulation to analyse the same event.

A proposed continuum of combination

Continuum of combination

In proposing a continuum of integrated research designs DePoy and Gitlin (1994) advocated that fully integrated designs sit at the top of a hierarchy, followed by mixed method strategies, followed by triangulation. Thus, DePoy and Gitlin (1994) see triangulation as the most basic form of integration and therefore at the low end of the hierarchy. Noting the numerous definitions in the literature, DePoy and Gitlin appear to define triangulation as a process that is used primarily within either quantitative or qualitative approaches. For example, according to DePoy and Gitlin (1994) triangulation might be used in a quantitative survey design, using two different scales to measure the same phenomenon, in order to achieve convergence across measures. Conversely, in a qualitative design a researcher might combine open-ended interviewing with direct observation to achieve a complete understanding of the phenomenon being studied. Thus, DePoy and Gitlin (1994) see triangulation as serving either a 'convergent function' or a 'completeness function', these being primarily within the same research approach.

With regard to 'mixed methods', the second level of the continuum, DePoy and Gitlin (1994) separate this into three basic strategies: a 'nested' strategy, a sequential approach and a parallel model. In using a nested strategy the researcher develops a study based on their own paradigmatic framework and then borrows specific techniques from another paradigm in an effort to strengthen an aspect of the study, for example, an ethnographic study that uses probability sampling to identify a representative sample (DePoy & Gitlin 1994). In using a sequential approach, the researcher may utilise in-depth interviewing in order to inform the construction of a tool for use in a quantitative study, or vice versa, a series of in-depth interviews may be used to follow up a survey questionnaire in order to clarify certain issues or concepts. Using a parallel model, the researcher (or researchers) utilise designs from qualitative and quantitative methods in a simultaneous fashion, acknowledging that they represent distinct ways of knowing, yet illuminating different aspects of the phenomenon under study (DePoy & Gitlin 1994).

Full integration represents the most complex form of integration and involves an enquiry that integrates multiple purposes and combines different strategies from different paradigms in order that each may contribute knowledge to a study of a single problem in order to derive a more complete understanding of the phenomenon (DePoy & Gitlin 1994). In this way, such integrated designs use the frameworks of distinct philosophical traditions to answer different questions within one study, for example, allowing the researcher to test an intervention using an experimental design, yet, through a qualitative design, permitting discovery of insights into the underlying process of change as a consequence of the intervention (DePoy & Gitlin 1994). This level of integration is innovative in that neither a qualitative or a quantitative design takes precedence over the other. This 'complementary' vision of research, according to DePoy and Gitlin (1994) is the most controversial. DePoy and Gitlin (1994) note some challenges for the fully integrated approach: the phenomena under investigation must be shown to warrant an integrated approach; ways of comparing and evaluating results must be systematically developed; and contradictions must be reconciled as they emerge during data collection and analysis. DePoy and Gitlin (1994) predicted that as more researchers participated in integrated designs, models would be developed to logically link diverse methods and causal and interpretive analyses.

Conclusion

It is apparent that the idea of combining research approaches is less controversial than previously thought and that this process is becoming increasingly popular in health and social care research, particularly within the nursing profession, but also within health services research in general (Dixon-Woods et al. 2005). However, it is also apparent that there is a lack of agreement with regard to the terminology used to describe such research. The concept of triangulation appears to be used in a number of ways and contexts, sometimes consistently but sometimes with distinct differences. For example, Kimchi et al.'s (1991) and Shih's (1998) usage of the term triangulation appear to be largely synonymous with DePoy and Gitlin's (1994) usage of the term 'full integration'. Clearly, we need to reach consensus on this matter, as well as developing ways of combining research approaches and methods in order to allow the full potential of integration. We also need to develop rigorous criteria for appraising and evaluating combined method research approaches. It is this issue, the appraisal of research evidence that the next chapter is concerned with.

Chapter 9
Critical appraisal

Introduction

This chapter explores and discusses the undertaking of critical appraisal, which refers to the process of evaluating the quality of research evidence.

Different levels of researcher undertake critical appraisal, ranging from students to professors. Some academic departments specialise in this, particularly with regard to undertaking systematic reviews and meta-analyses (these will be returned to later in this chapter). Commercial organisations, such as pharmaceutical companies also undertake critical appraisal, for example, in order to assess the requirements of the marketplace.

However, given the proliferation of evidence-based practice, as noted in Chapter 2, the ability to evaluate published evidence about the accuracy of specific diagnostic tests and the efficacy of specific interventions, preventions or therapies is perceived as an important skill for health and social care professionals. Therefore, such practitioners need to be able to demonstrate critical appraisal skills requiring the use of appropriate tools and to comment on the overall quality of the evidence resulting from research and how far the evidence goes towards addressing or informing their area of interest.

The ability to analyse and synthesise the research evidence which underpins professional practice, enables practitioners to critically evaluate the potential contribution of a variety of research methods in answering health and social care research questions. Importantly, as noted in Chapter 6, the conclusions arrived at by the authors of literature that has been critically reviewed need to be evaluated with regard to feasibility, validity and appropriateness. Despite this, training in assessing the design, conduct and interpretation of clinical research generally receives little attention. This can leave health and social care practitioners poorly equipped to perform worthwhile critical appraisal and to apply the results of published research to their practice. Practitioners and students are increasingly being required to critically analyse material and evaluate other people's work in an organised, systematic manner to determine how worthy, useful or important it is. Thus, the following sections of this chapter offer advice on the main considerations when undertaking a critique. It should be noted that the guidelines for critiquing research are generally separated into qualitative and quantitative checklists, because, as the previous chapter highlighted, there is still lack of consensus on guidelines for critiquing combined approach research. However, it should become apparent that some of the general points presented below will be applicable to both quantitative and qualitative approaches.

General principles

Generally, a critique should start by attempting to explain the purpose of the article. Key questions that could be posed are:

- Does the author say for whom they are writing?
- Is there a need for this article?
- Why is the article important/topical?

Critical appraisal should summarise the main arguments, giving a straightforward factual account of what the writer is saying. It should examine the theoretical approach on which the article is based. This section is important and the ability to critically analyse the piece of writing must be demonstrated. It is also important that in reading the article in preparation for the critique one should continue to ask why the author is saying what they are saying. Is it correct, relevant, complete and fair? The critique should also include the reader's own assessment of the value and validity of the article as a contribution to their profession, backed up with evidence from the article and from other sources.

Critical appraisal

A good critical appraisal should consider the following general points:

- Have issues of bias been considered?
- What assumptions has the author made about the readers?
- What sort of article is it? For example, is it research or a review?
- What method was used and was it appropriate?
- Has the author achieved their objective, if stated, or what is it that the author meant to achieve?
- Are the conclusions/views of the author supported by the critical appraisal?
- Is the author attempting to stimulate debate – if so, is that appropriate?
- Is there sufficient reference to available literature?
- Has the literature been well integrated into the text?
- Is the text well justified in using other work or does it read as the author's opinion?
- Are all relevant concepts and variables included in the review?
- Is there evidence that the work is unbiased?
- Was the work original? If not, did it still constitute an important addition to knowledge?
- Was the study design feasible/sensible/appropriate?
- What outcomes were chosen and how were they measured?
- Who was in the study, how were they selected and recruited?
- Who was included, who was excluded and why?
- Was the study undertaken in a realistic (true to life setting) or was it in a highly controlled environment?
- Did the study include information on those participants who dropped out – for example, the reasons why?
- Was it stated that research ethics committee approval was acquired?

In critiquing a paper, one's writing should be bold and views clearly stated. However, one should beware of making sweeping statements and generalities, remembering always to substantiate opinions. In stating opinions about the strengths and weaknesses of an article one should be able to explain and justify the underlying reasons.

Research issues in health and social care

There is a requirement to assess in some depth the particular methods used to undertake the research in order to generate evidence, in this way evaluating the design and process of the research. This needs to take place in addition to evaluating the outcomes (findings, conclusions) arrived at by the authors of the critiqued literature, which will also need to be evaluated with regard to feasibility, validity and appropriateness. Thus, it is necessary to comment on the appropriateness of the methodology used and on any perceived strengths and weaknesses of particular methods including how outcome measures were chosen, how they were actually measured and any statistical tests applied to data. It is also necessary to comment on the overall quality, generalisability and the applicability of the evidence to practitioner's particular area of practice, that is, to what extent the findings could adequately inform practice and in particular, adequately inform evidence-based practice.

When experienced in critical appraisal, it may be possible to comment as to whether additional research in an area may be required and to suggest in general terms how this research may be carried out in the future. For example, the feasibility of such work, whether it needs to be qualitative, quantitative, combined method, who might do it, whether it should be collaborative (i.e. multidisciplinary) and who might be expected to fund this work.

Newman *et al.* (2005) reiterate that critical appraisal is about deciding whether or not to use particular research findings to inform decision making within practice. It involves assessing the quality of research reports and judging the extent to which any flaws might affect the study results. It is then possible to weigh up whether the findings reported are strong (trustworthy) enough to warrant altering current practice.

While several sets of guidelines are available to facilitate the process (some of these are presented below), Newman *et al.* (2005) advise that critical appraisal skills should not be represented merely as a set of techniques that can be worked through and ticked off on a checklist to elicit a definitive answer about the trustworthiness of a piece of research. Rather, critical appraisal skills are about taking a questioning and considered approach to research publications. This means assessing research reports with a critical eye and not simply accepting the word of the authors. According to Newman *et al.* (2005) the critically appraising practitioner routinely asks: 'Is this research trustworthy enough that I feel comfortable using it to inform my practice decision making?' This involves examining the research for potential bias and considering how this may impact on the results reported (Newman *et al.* 2005).

Having outlined some general points to consider when critically appraising research, the following sections look at critical appraisal of specific types of research articles.

Critically appraising quantitative research articles

Quantitative research articles

This section revisits some of the concepts encountered in Chapter 5 on analysis of quantitative data and aims to give a basic insight into some of the functions encountered in quantitative analysis where the design may be a survey or of an experimental nature with numerical data.

Within the findings of any study, there will be a range of results, from one extreme to another. This is called a distribution and commonly there will be an increased number of results somewhere around the middle of the range. This is known as a normal distribution. The average value (as mentioned in Chapter 4) that has the greatest number of subjects is known as the mean (please see below). A distribution is often depicted in graphical form.

Mean: A measure of the central tendency around which most values lie.

Standard Deviation: The value of the standard deviation gives an indication of the spread of a distribution around the mean.

Median: The central point of a distribution

Mode: The value that occurs most often

Once data have been collected it is necessary to make some sense of it and there are two main ways of undertaking this:

Descriptive Analysis: Remember that descriptive statistics can be useful in making straightforward observations about data as it is presented. This is commonly done in relation to the distribution of results which may be shown graphically, although such data may often lack the power to make inferences about a data set.

Inferential Analysis: We may want to be able to infer something about the data that we have collected. It is important to remember that when trying to determine the influence of independent variables on dependent variables it is possible to either compare two or more groups to see if they are different from each other, or to determine whether two or more ranges of values either influence or correlate with each other. This is done by applying a test to the data in the form of a mathematical equation, which will yield a result. The test chosen will depend on the type of data that we have and a table of some examples is provided in Chapter 5, Table 5.5. Fortunately, nowadays, this can be done using a computer program which takes a lot of the hard work out of it.

Remember, as was discussed in Chapter 5, the type of test chosen will depend on the nature of the dependent variable, that is, whether you have counted (nominal), ordered (ordinal) or measured (interval and ratio) data. When these statistical tests are carried out the objective is to determine whether the result is significant or not (does it actually mean something?). Thus, when a comparison is undertaken you are seeking to determine whether there is a statistical difference between the groups. As noted in earlier chapters the test applied will normally provide this information in the form of a 'p' value.

'P' Value

As discussed in Chapter 5, basically, the 'p' value indicates the probability that a result is significant. Normally, we want to be sure with a certain degree of confidence that a result is significant. That degree of confidence is usually 95%. In other words, we want to be more than 95% certain that we have a significant result, or less than 5% certain that we do not have a significant result. This is translated into $p < 0.05$, indicating a significant result.

You will regularly see 'p' values reported in published studies and they usually work at the 95% level, but they may be used at 99% in, for example, the case of a drug trial where it is much more important to be sure about what the results indicate. In this case you would see $p < 0.01$.

There are many different ways of showing things and many different tests that can be applied, but it is important to remember that these basic premises apply. It is not necessary to be a statistician in order to carry out or to appraise basic research statistics. What is needed is to understand the mechanism by which decisions can be reached. To facilitate this, several tools are presented below to aid the critical appraisal of quantitative research articles.

Observing that medical practice is increasingly dependent on mathematics (as is evidence-based practice in other fields of health and social care), Greenhalgh (1997a) developed a list of questions to assist in appraising the statistical validity of a research paper, as follows:

- Have the authors determined whether groups are comparable and if necessary adjusted for baseline differences? Differences in age, sex etc. can cause bias.
- What data have they collected and have they used appropriate statistical tests?
- Were data analysed according to the original research protocol? Or, were different tests used because the authors could not demonstrate significance with the planned testing?
- Was there justification provided for any obscure statistical tests?
- Were outlying results (results deemed to be far removed from 'normal' values) taken into consideration?
- Was a two-tailed test used when the effect of an intervention could conceivably be a negative one?

Terminology box

Two-tailed test

Instead of making an assumption that measurements will lie within a particular range, for example that blood pressure will always rise when people stop taking morphine, we should also test to determine whether blood pressure may fall. In this way we will be testing to determine whether low or high results have arisen by chance. However, the cut off point for statistical significance is higher in a two-tailed test because we are looking at both ends of the range of data, so if we are testing at the $p < 0.05$ level we will be splitting our 5% probability in two, that is 2.5% at each end of the range.

Critically appraising randomised controlled trials (RCTs)

The Centre for Appraisal Skills Programme (CASP 2005) have developed a list of questions to help you make sense of RCTs. The first two questions are for screening purposes. If the answer to either one of them is 'no' then the trustworthiness of the study is questionable and it is probably not worth investing the time, trouble and effort to continue reading the paper.

- Was there a clearly focused research question?
- Was this a true RCT and was it appropriate to undertake one?
- Was there appropriate allocation to intervention and control groups?
- Was there blinding?
- Were all participants accounted for at the conclusion of the study?
- Were all participants followed up and data collected in the same way?
- Were there enough participants to minimise chance?
- Was there an appropriate calculation to determine the sample size?
- How were findings presented? What was the main result?
- How precise are the results? Were they precise enough to enable a decision?
- Were confidence intervals reported?
- Would any decision to use the tested intervention be the same at both the upper and lower confidence limits?
- Are all important outcomes considered in order to apply results?
- Are the results generalisable? Can you provide the same treatment or intervention in your setting?
- Are outcomes relevant or appropriate for the individual, family, policy makers, professionals, the wider community?

Confidence Intervals

The confidence interval is something that enables us to calculate from the mean average of a sample what the mean averages of other samples would be, assuming that the data are normally distributed, that is, 68% of the sample values are within plus or minus one standard deviation (SD) of the mean, indicating the mean average is a true representation of the central value. After calculating the standard error (SE), as was done above for the *t*-test, it is assumed that 95% of other samples of people who can be matched for age, sex, bodyweight etc., will have means within two SEs of the sample mean from which you are calculating. This is based on a statistical concept known as the central limit theorem, although it is beyond the scope of this book to provide a detailed account of this theorem. However, using the central limit theorem it is possible to calculate the confidence interval for these samples. Thus, using our sample from the BP study, with a mean of 134 and a SE of 3.1, we can estimate that 95% of other similar, sample means will be within 134 plus or minus 6.2, giving us a 95% confidence interval (CI) of 127.8 to 140.2 for blood pressure.

The Centre for Evidence-based Social Services has a number of tools to aid working through different research papers or reports (Newman *et al.* 2005). Below are questions to help in appraising the quality, trustworthiness and relevance of RCTs. As with the CASP questions, the first two questions are for screening purposes. Once again, if the answer to either one of them is 'no' then the trustworthiness of the study is questionable and it is probably not worth investing the time, trouble and effort to continue reading the paper.

- Were there clear aims?
- Was an RCT most appropriate to answer the question?
- Was there true random allocation?
- Was allocation concealed from those in and running the study?
- Was there blinding?
- Were intervention and control groups well matched?
- Was the sample size justified?
- Was there an appropriate calculation to determine the sample size?
- Was follow-up data collected in the same way?
- Were all participants accounted for at the end? Were any drop outs different?
- Were the results clearly presented and appropriate?
- Were conclusions supported by the results?
- Were ethical issues considered?
- Was the study relevant to clients and/or practice?

It is clear from the above guidelines for critically appraising quantitative research that there is general agreement on several aspects, although Greenhalgh (1997a, b) tends to focus more on the pragmatics of statistical testing.

Systematic review and meta-analysis

Systematic review and meta-analysis

While RCTs are considered to be primary research studies within the quantitative approach, you may remember from earlier chapters that systematic reviewing is also an important form of secondary quantitative research and that a meta-analysis is a particular type of systematic review. These two types of study also have specific areas that need particular attention when undertaking critical appraisal and thus, accordingly there are specific guidelines.

Systematic reviewing involves the unbiased collection, critical appraisal and synthesis of relevant studies on a topic. Therefore, if you undertake a critical appraisal of a systematic review you will in effect be appraising the appraisers and this is a perfectly feasible and acceptable undertaking, as nobody is perfect! The general process of undertaking a systematic review is as follows:

- posing a question
- doing a literature search
- applying inclusion/exclusion criteria to papers
- reviewing the selected literature
- overview of primary studies that used explicit, reproducible methods
- imposition of relevant, desirable outcomes
- benchmarking
- quality filtering.

A meta-analysis can be described as follows:

- a systematic review that uses statistical methods to combine and summarise the results of several studies
- mathematical synthesis of primary trials/studies that addressed the same hypothesis in the same way
- systematic scoring.

Tools used for scoring include:

- Number Needed to Treat (an example of how to calculate this was given in Chapter 4)
- Number Needed to Harm.

A meta-analysis can determine success or failure of a product, for example, a newly developed drug.

Systematic reviewers and meta-analysts use stringent inclusion and exclusion criteria when deciding on which studies to review. Some considerations are as follows:

- appropriate statistical testing
- elimination of bias
- randomisation/blinding
- sample – number and type of study subjects
- withdrawals and adverse events
- methods of data collection – valid, reliable?
- relevant outcomes – client/patient-orientated outcomes
- statistical significance of findings
- cost/benefit ratio
- benefit/harm ratio.

However, when appraising and reviewing the systematic reviewers it is useful to consider the following points:

- Quality of the review question
- Quality of the literature search
- Quality of inclusion/exclusion criteria
- Quality of the assessment of studies
- Was it feasible to combine data?
- Was there clear numerical expression of results?
- Were the findings relevant to practice?

Greenhalgh (1997c) defines a systematic review as an overview of primary studies that used explicit and reproducible methods. Meta-analysis is defined as a mathematical synthesis of the results of two or more primary studies that addressed the same hypothesis in the same way (Greenhalgh 1997c). Although meta-analysis can increase the precision of a result, it is important to ensure that the methods used for the review were valid and reliable. Greenhalgh lists some advantages of the systematic review process as follows:

- Explicit methods limit bias in identifying and rejecting studies.
- Conclusions are more accurate and reliable.
- Large amounts of information can be assimilated quickly by practitioners, researchers and policy-makers.
- Delay between research discoveries and implementation of effective diagnostic and therapeutic strategies may be reduced.
- Results of different studies can be formally compared to establish generalisability of findings and consistency of results.
- Reasons for inconsistency in results across studies can be identified and new hypotheses generated about particular subgroups.
- Quantitative systematic reviews can increase the precision of the overall result.

Accordingly, Greenhalgh (1997c) advises the evaluation of systematic review by asking the following questions:

- Can you find an important question that the review addressed? It needs to be defined very precisely.
- Was a thorough search done of the appropriate databases and were other potentially important sources explored? For example, foreign authors, references, unpublished, raw data?
- Was methodological quality assessed and the studies weighted accordingly? Was there good quality design and conduct, was a scoring system used to select appropriate studies (for example, the Jadad *et al.* (1996) scoring system for RCTs)? Was the likelihood of random errors assessed? What was the width of any confidence interval? Were the findings generalisable to a particular target population?
- How sensitive were the results to the way in which the review was carried out?
- Was there evidence of exclusion of trials with a negative result?
- Have numerical results been interpreted with common sense and due regard to broader aspects of the problem?
- Should a numerical result influence the care of an individual patient?

Greenhalgh (1997c) advocates that a well executed meta-analysis is easier for a non-statistician to understand than a stack of primary research papers. Furthermore, reading a meta-analysis cuts down the labour of going through each individual methods and results section of primary papers. Thus, the meta-analyst's job is to tabulate relevant information, including study inclusion criteria, sample size, baseline characteristics, withdrawal rate from the study and the results of endpoints (outcomes).

The Centre for Appraisal Skills Programme (CASP) also produce a list of questions to help you make sense of reviews. Once again, the first two questions are for screening purposes. If the answer to either question is 'no' then the trustworthiness of the study is questionable and it is probably not worth investing the time, trouble and effort to continue reading the paper.

- Was there a clearly focused question?
- Were the appropriate type of studies included?
- Was there an attempt to identify all relevant studies? Which databases, reference lists, experts were consulted? Was there a search for unpublished work or for non-English language studies?
- Was there an assessment of the quality of studies? Was there a clear predetermined strategy, a scoring system, more than one assessor?
- If the results of studies were combined, was it reasonable to do so?
- How were the findings presented? What is the main result?
- What is the size of the result? How meaningful is it?
- How would you sum up the bottom line in one sentence?
- How precise are the results? Are they precise enough to make a decision? Is there a confidence interval reported? Is there a 'p' value reported?
- Can the results be applied to your local population?
- Can you provide the same treatment/intervention in your setting?
- Were all important outcomes considered in order to apply results?
- Are the results generalisable?
- Are outcomes relevant or appropriate for the individual, family,

policy makers, professionals, or the wider community?

- Should policy or practice change as a result of the evidence contained in the review?
- Does any benefit outweigh harm or cost? If this information is not reported, can it be found elsewhere?

With regard to systematic reviews, meta-analyses and statistical testing in general, Greenhalgh (1997c) suggests an additional list of things to bear in mind as follows:

- Have 'p' values been calculated and interpreted appropriately?
- Why make a question of effectiveness of intervention a yes/no dichotomy? Are there points in between, such as on a continuum as represented by the confidence interval?
- Have confidence intervals been calculated, and do the author's conclusions reflect them?
- Remember that the confidence interval indicates the limits within which the 'real' difference between the intervention effect is likely to lie and hence the strength of the inference from the result. The narrower the confidence interval the more accurate the results.
- Have assumptions been made about the nature and direction of causality? For example, because a town has high number of unemployed and a high crime rate, it does not mean that the unemployed are committing crimes.
- The bottom line – have the authors expressed the effects of an intervention in terms of the likely benefit or harm which an individual client/patient can expect?
- Statistically significant results may not be clinically significant.
- It is all very well to say that a particular intervention produces a 'statistically significant' difference, but it would be better to know how much the chance of good outcome would be improved by the intervention.

According to Greenhalgh (1997d), four calculations can answer this last point:

- Relative risk reduction
- Absolute risk reduction

- NNT (please see Chapter 4 for a calculation of this)
- Odds ratio.

Example of relative risk reduction, absolute risk reduction, odds ratio

A group of researchers found that pathological gambling occurred in 1.5% (8 out of 529 people) of Parkinson's patients treated with pramipexole, this occurring in people who had never gambled previously (Driver-Dunckley *et al.* 2003). While the findings do not indicate that this problem occurs frequently among people with Parkinson's disease and most people treated with pramipexole experience no such effect, it would appear that there is an increased likelihood of gambling associated with taking pramipexole. However, the drug company that makes pramipexole claims that compulsive gambling is a symptom of Parkinson's disease anyway.

In an imaginary scenario, let's say that the said drug company produced data from another group of Parkinson's patients who were not taking pramipexole that demonstrated a prevalence of 0.375% (2 out of 529) for pathological gambling, again occurring in people who had never gambled previously. We could then calculate the risk of becoming a pathological gambler if we took pramipexole, compared to if we did not. The risk of becoming a pathological gambler when taking pramipexole is 1.5%, the risk of becoming one when not taking it is 0.375%. To calculate the relative risk we divide 0.375% by 1.5% giving us 0.25 (25%).

Therefore the following applies:

- The relative risk reduction of becoming a pathological gambler when not taking pramipexole would be 25% in these people.
- The absolute risk reduction when not taking pramipexole would be 1.5% minus 0.375% which is 1.25%.
- The odds ratio (which ironically, gamblers are almost always interested in) would be 8/529 divided by 2/529, that is, 0.015/0.00375 = 4.

Accordingly, when provided with such figures it is possible for practitioners to make informed decisions about whether to prescribe a particular type of treatment or not.

Other checklists

Greenhalgh (1997d, e) provides two other lists of points to bear in mind, one regarding how to read papers that report drug trials and one comprising questions to ask about an economic analysis. These are presented below.

Drug trials

- Danger of uncontrolled studies, the placebo effect.
- The need for reputable, independent studies; the need to ignore anecdotal evidence, such as a particular well known person is already using this drug.
- A new product not always better merely because it is new.
- Value of the drug needs to be expressed in terms of safety, tolerability, efficacy and price (STEP).
- Drug efficacy should be measured in terms of clinical endpoints that are relevant to patients. Surrogate end points (such as elevation of an enzyme in blood which is associated with improvement of a condition – serum marker, pharmacokinetic measurement – blood concentrations of drug, in vitro measurements) should be valid and a true predictor of disease or risk thereof and should have acceptable negative predictive value (of being not at risk), changes in such markers should rapidly reflect response to treatment.
- Promotional literature of low scientific value should not be allowed to influence prescribing decisions.

Economic analysis

- Is the analysis based on a study that answers a clearly defined (clinical) question about an economically important issue?
- Whose viewpoint are costs and benefits being considered from?
- Have the interventions that are being compared been shown to be (clinically) effective?
- Are the interventions sensible and workable in the settings where they are likely to be applied?
- Which method of analysis was used and was this appropriate?
- How were costs and benefits measured?
- Were incremental rather than absolute benefits considered?
- Was 'here and now' given precedence over the distant future?

- Was a sensitivity analysis performed? For example, was any required equipment costed?
- Were 'bottom line' aggregate scores overused?

Appraising quantitative research: considerations

In view of the above guidelines and checklists and their similarities and differences in appraising quantitative research studies, the following general considerations are pertinent.

- Is the research question valid?
- Has bias potential been minimised?
- Are all the participants and outcomes reported?
- Have there been losses over the course of the study?
- Is the sample studied representative of the population which the results will be inferred to?
- Beware of small sample studies only reported as percentages, or percentages from sub groups combined.
- Previous research that is cited as evidence in current papers but that would not be admissible today, for example, research that was undertaken without ethical approval, that was conducted using prisoners, or that involved coerced responses, should be treated with caution.
- References should be checked to ensure that findings have not been inferred to humans from studies on animals, that sample sizes are adequate and that findings from relatively small samples have not been cited to convey the impression that an idea or concept is universally accepted.
- Check terminology – addiction rate may be based on studies reporting abuse rates; the definition of terms varies.

Validity and reliability

Validity and reliability

One last point to remember, as discussed in Chapter 4, is that quantitative research measures may not always be tested for validity and reliability, usually due to lack of resources including time and money. However, this does not mean that these measures are inaccurate or inconsistent, just that these aspects are not known. The point to bear in mind when critically appraising such research reports is that if validity and reliability testing are not mentioned then it can be assumed that this testing has not been undertaken. Remember that validity pertains to the degree to which a measure actually measures what it purports to be measuring. Reliability is concerned with the overall consistency of a measure. Also remember that while validity and reliability are related, there are important differences. It is possible to have a measure that is reliable but not valid, because a test can be consistently wrong and consistently wrong by the same amount. However, it is not possible to have a valid test that is not reliable, because it could not then be considered as accurate.

Critically appraising qualitative research articles

As was mentioned in previous chapters, qualitative research can be undervalued and perceived to be of less worth than quantitative studies (Grypdonck 2006). This can be because readers do not understand how to assess the value of such work. Indeed, qualitative work may be seen as subjective, or 'woolly', if the methodology and the rigour with which the study was undertaken are not adequately explained. As was also mentioned in previous chapters, qualitative research does not try to 'count' or 'measure' in the same way as statistical studies, therefore different appraisal techniques are required.

Qualitative research aims to understand social phenomena within natural settings and to emphasise the meanings, experiences and opinions of participants. Qualitative studies try to answer 'what', 'why' and 'how', instead of 'how many'. Qualitative studies then aim to provide rich description and interpretation across a holistic area. As has been discussed earlier, there are a number of research methods which are considered to be 'qualitative' and different ways of collecting qualitative data. Therefore, this section only gives a general overview of issues to consider in qualitative critiques and some guidelines are presented and discussed.

Sampling and method are important aspects of making value

statements about a qualitative article. Methodology can be strengthened by using a combination of methods (as discussed in the previous chapter) and by using other researchers to independently analyse the data collected and it is important that issues of bias are considered. With regard to qualitative studies it is still appropriate to ask:

- Is the study valid?
- Is the study important?
- Can I apply this study to my practice?

Greenhalgh and Taylor (1997) have outlined a series of questions which can be used to appraise qualitative research as follows:

- Did the paper describe an important problem addressed via a clearly formulated question?
- Was a qualitative approach appropriate?
- How were the setting and the subjects selected?
- What was the researcher's perspective, and has this been taken into account?
- What methods did the researcher use for collecting data, and are these described in enough detail?
- What methods did the researcher use to analyse the data, and what quality control measures were implemented?
- Are the results credible, and if so, are they important?
- What conclusions were drawn, and are they justified by the results?
- Are the findings of the study transferable to other settings?

The Centre for Evidence-based Social Services offers the following guide (Newman *et al.* 2005). If the answer to one of the first two questions is 'no', then the trustworthiness of the study is questionable and it is probably not worth investing the time, trouble and effort to continue reading the paper.

- Were the aims of the study clear?
- Was qualitative research the right approach to answer the research question?
- Was the research design the most appropriate? What was used? Interviews? Observation?

- Was the sampling strategy clear/appropriate? How were participants selected?
- Was the sample size justified? Was data saturation reached?
- Did the method of data collection fit with the aims of the study? Where did data collection take place? By whom and how? How long did it take?
- Was data collection systematic? Was it collected in the same way for all participants? Is it clear how data were analysed? Were they coded, themed? Was it discourse analysis? Grounded theory?
- Were the results clearly presented and appropriate? Was it clear how any themes were derived?
- Was there a sufficient amount of original data to support interpretations and conclusions?
- Were data not supporting findings discussed?
- Were steps taken to increase trustworthiness? Was there respondent validation? Was there triangulation? Did a colleague check interpretation?
- Was there critical examination of the researcher's own role, bias and influence?
- Were ethical issues addressed? Was research ethics committee approval acquired?
- Were participants given clear information? Did they give informed consent?
- Was confidentiality/anonymity assured?
- Is there any relevance to one's own clients/practice?

Likewise, the Centre for Appraisal Skills Programme (CASP 2005) also provide questions to help you make sense of qualitative research. This includes the standard screening questions; if the answer to one of the first two questions is 'no' then the trustworthiness of the study is questionable and it is probably not worth investing the time, trouble and effort to continue reading the paper.

- Was there a clear statement of aims?
- Was the methodology appropriate?

- Was the research design the most appropriate?
- Was the recruitment strategy appropriate to the aims? Was it explained to participants why they were selected? Is there an account of why some may have declined to take part?
- Were data collected in a way that addressed the research issue?
- What was the setting? What were the methods? Were they clear and justified? Was there saturation?
- Was the relationship between researcher and participants considered?
- Were ethical issues considered?
- Was there rigorous data analysis?
- Was there a clear statement of findings?
- How valuable is the research?

While there is no one definitive list for appraising qualitative studies and written articles of qualitative work, the above lists give an idea of what the important criteria are and how you can begin to go beyond reading a paper purely for interest. It is reasonable to say that the strength of the qualitative approach lies largely in validity, that is how closely the study measures what it claims to measure – how close the results are to reality. Well-conducted qualitative research should get to the heart of an issue – it should explore what is really going on. As you read qualitative papers you should question what is being said, question any claims being made, look for evidence to back up conclusions and relate the article to other similar published articles – then you will be beginning to critique and appraise qualitative research (Greenhalgh & Taylor 1997).

Appraising qualitative research: general considerations

Qualitative methods aim to make sense of concepts with regard to the meanings people attach to them. They emphasise uniqueness, richness and diversity of human experience. They may develop/refine primary research questions for quantitative research. Qualitative evidence/findings can also be evaluated using reproducible methods. However, this extends beyond evaluation that uses a set of rules. But there are some basic guidelines:

- Was a qualitative approach appropriate?
- Was the chosen approach thorough?
- How was the setting selected?
- How were the participants selected?
- Were accounts from participants who were more articulate or accessible given more credibility?
- What was the researcher's perspective, if it was considered?
- Was the relationship between researcher and participants fully considered and/or described?
- Was there separation of the researcher's own experience from the participant's?
- Was the 'truth' participant or researcher orientated?
- Were data collection methods adequate?
- Were methods adequately described?
- What quality control measures were implemented?
- How well are the findings presented?
- How credible are the findings?
- How meaningful are the findings?
- How relevant are the findings to practice?
- Are the conclusions justified by the findings?

Collecting data, coding and categorising it, writing memos to oneself about emerging ideas and concepts, determining a core category, constantly recycling through the various stages of the procedure to eventually generate a cogent theory is challenging to say the least. Consequently, it is not surprising that when critiquing research that the authors claim is using a grounded theory approach, it is found that the method was limited primarily to the utilisation of analytical procedures and does not generate any new or substantive theory (Priest *et al.* 2002).

Conclusion

Despite the earlier statement that critical appraisal is not just about ticking off items on a list, this chapter has introduced a number of such checklists to aid the choice of criteria for critical appraisal of research articles. In addition to these checklists, when undertaking critical appraisal, the following broad issues should be considered.

The paper needs to be trustworthy. The results should be considered in the context of other work done in the area and need to be applicable to your health/social care setting. Are limitations of the study acknowledged? How compelling was the evidence? Do the findings constitute evidence to inform practice and will they be likely to contribute to the update of health and social care practice? Remember that no piece of research is likely to be perfect and inevitably there will be a compromise between the ideal design and practicalities. Also bear in mind that if you cannot understand the paper, it may be unwise to automatically assume the author is cleverer than you; indeed, you could assume that the author lacks the ability to convey what they mean.

It has been noted earlier in this book that knowledge systems represent complex series of values, assumptions and methodological rules governing what might constitute appropriate knowledge in a given time and place. Therefore, in critically appraising research evidence we need to bear in mind that all knowledge, and therefore evidence, is grounded in historical and social circumstances and that cultural or moral values may be translated into 'scientific facts'. The researcher's values are always at play, both in developing research studies or in interpreting the findings of these studies.

Remember to consider how the research is linked to theory in general terms. For example, whether it appears to be theory testing research or theory generating research. It is also important to consider the theoretical framework (if any) that the authors are operating within and not to automatically assume that this is an appropriate one. Are the authors using a stated framework merely as 'window dressing', to give the study a degree of legitimacy that it would not otherwise have? Conversely, if there is no apparent framework, consider whether there needs to be one.

As noted in Chapter 5 on interpretation of research findings, with regard to authors' conclusions, bear in mind that these conclusions should be appropriate, valid and relevant to the question and/or aim of the research and should be based on the findings and the analysis of data. Remember to be wary of reports written by parties with vested interests as these are likely to contain overstatements, unsubstantiated connections or explanations and results that are inappropriately generalised beyond the scope of the study. Also, beware of authors' own views expressed in the absence of appropriate supporting evidence, as in some cases, when it is not possible to identify cause and effect, researchers often interpret this for themselves.

Finally, and not least, try to consider the ethical implications of the research, not just whether research ethics committee approval was granted for the study, but any wider ranging ethical implications. These issues will be discussed in more detail in Chapter 11 on research governance and ethics.

The following chapter focuses on how to compile a piece of research-based writing. It will be helpful when working through the next chapter, to contemplate the issues raised in this chapter and to be mindful that those reading your research writing might well be applying any number of the critical appraisal tools and criteria that have been introduced in this chapter.

Chapter 10
Research writing

Introduction

The process of research writing pertains not only to the writing of research papers or research reports but also to the writing of research proposals, applications for research funding, research protocols and research ethics committee applications (research ethics will be discussed in more detail in the next chapter on research governance and research ethics). The requirements for all the aforementioned documents include similar elements. For example, all will need to have some kind of introduction and background section setting the research into context and all will need to end with some kind of a summary and conclusion section. Other examples of similarities are that the methods section of a research proposal will be identical to the methods section in a research protocol, or an application to a funding body; the methods section in a research ethics committee application will be a similar, yet abbreviated version of that in a research proposal or protocol. Also, some ethics committees may require a full research proposal of 2000 to 3000 words in addition to the standard application form.

However, it is common for different organisations and institutions to require research writing to be presented in differing formats. For example, university students will find that in addition to having to adhere to a specified word limit they are required to use a particular referencing system such as Harvard (where the author's name and year of publication is cited within the text) or Vancouver (where only a number is cited in the text, which is matched to the same number in the reference list). Some university research assignment formats will require the use of specific headings for each section, some will not.

Research issues in health and social care

Various professional journals have their own specifications with regard to how manuscripts should be submitted, including a specified referencing system, a required number and sequence of sections and a specified word limit. Research protocols will often need to be written in a particular format; for example, a drug company may have specific criteria for their clinical drug trial protocols and ethics committees will have their own requirements as to how the research protocol or methods section within an application for committee approval should be presented. Those who apply for research funding from bodies such as the Economic and Social Research Council or the Medical Research Council, will also find that they are required to structure their applications in a particular way.

In view of the above, while this chapter primarily focuses on the process of writing up and presenting a research paper or report, it should become apparent that the techniques used in undertaking this exercise are readily transferable to the other general types of research writing mentioned. For example, if one has had a paper published reporting on a particular research study and is intending to apply for funding for future, larger studies of the same nature, it will be feasible to 'cut and paste' various sections of the published paper, such as the introduction setting the research area in context, into the application for funding. Similarly it is possible to use the format of the methods section in a research proposal to inform the methods section when writing the report after the research has been completed. One may simply change the tense, from describing what one intended to do in the proposal, to what one actually did in the study, obviously, not forgetting to include any particular modifications that may have been necessary in executing the study.

Writing up research

Writing up research

The following sections of this chapter introduce the suggested sections for writing a research report or paper. As indicated in acknowledging the abovementioned different requirements for research writing, the following sections need not be seen as representing hard and fast rules, rather as general guidelines which can be modified accordingly.

Research writing

The general format and sequence of sections used in this chapter for writing up research will be presented as follows:

- Title
- Abstract (this may not always be required)
- Introduction
- Background
- Research question/hypothesis
- Operationalisation of terminology
- Literature review
- Method
- Results
- Discussion
- Conclusion
- References.

Title

Your title should comprise a concise, succinct and clear description of your research. It should inform the reader what the study is about. You should avoid using tautologies (using additional and unnecessary words to describe the same thing), being verbose (using too many words in general) and you should endeavour not to mislead the reader, for example by exaggerating the worthiness of the contents of the paper.

Abstract

Sometimes it will be necessary to write an 'abstract' of your research. For example if you are writing a paper for submission to a journal for publication or writing a dissertation for academic purposes, you will be required to produce a summary of your study to provide the reader with a preview. This is usually between 150 and 250 words. In your abstract it will be necessary to describe the central topic and research question or hypothesis, how and why the study was undertaken, who and how many people were studied, using what sampling technique, what methods were utilised, how the data were analysed and what the conclusion was. In essence, you are summarising why you did the study, how you did it, what happened and what the implications are. This is no mean feat, considering that you may have to condense several thousand words into such a short section. Some students make the mistake of trying to write the abstract first because this is where it will sit in sequential order after the title. However, it is advisable to write the abstract last, after all the other sections have been completed and can be referred to in order to inform the abstract. This may seem obvious to some, but it is surprising how many times one sees an abstract that does not adequately describe the study, because it was written before various modifications were made and then the author did not remember to alter the abstract accordingly.

Introduction

This is where you introduce what you propose to do. Mention your subject area or area of practice and the problem or interest within this area that has come to your attention along with the overall aims and objectives that underpin your reasons for undertaking the research. You can also mention the significance (not the statistical significance) and potential contribution of the study to the relevant area.

Background

It may be possible to combine background information into an expanded introduction section. However, it is also feasible to follow on from the introduction with a specific background section in which you describe the research area, problem or interest in enough detail as to provide justification for the study and an explanation to those who may not be overly familiar with the area.

Research question or hypothesis

While it may be possible to include your research question in the introduction or background section, it is helpful to the reader to 'signpost' the clearly stated research question, that is, a statement of purpose about what you are trying to find out, or your hypothesis. You could also describe how the research question came about in relation to the aims and objectives and how it fits within the research area. Please remember, as was highlighted in Chapter 3 on developing a research question, that the research question is simply a question that you seek to answer through the study and that a hypothesis is something that is to be tested by the study. It should also be remembered that usage of the term 'hypothesis' in this context differs from the wider usage we sometimes come across in various other forms of literature, where reference to a hypothesis may be synonymous with describing a theory or belief.

Terminology box

Research question

A research question is simply a question that you seek to answer through the proposed study. Research questions should elicit an answer that may: describe, explain, identify, qualify, substantiate or predict something. The findings should be able to generate new evidence, add to existing evidence, generate or modify theory, and ideally, have the potential to improve practice.

Terminology box

Hypothesis

While it was noted earlier that quantitative research does not necessarily entail testing a hypothesis, when conducting an experiment it is seen as standard practice to start with a theory and from this theory to generate a hypothesis to test. Remember, this process is described as falsificationist, whereby the findings of the experiment either support or refute the hypothesis. However, we can never be 100% sure the findings are true because there is always the possibility that our results are due to chance. Therefore, statistical testing of the significance of our results is used to determine the probability of our results being due to chance. If our statistical test indicates that the probability of our findings being due to chance is higher than 5%, in this case we would say that our hypothesis is not supported and therefore we cannot reject the 'null hypothesis'.

Operationalisation of terminology

As noted in Chapter 3, it is important to avoid ambiguity and to define your terms clearly. Therefore, it is useful to have a section where you define your terms quite early on. Give clear definitions of any obscure or uncommon terms used, or where there is the potential for ambiguity or misinterpretation. For example, you can state the following: 'For the purposes of this study certain terms are defined as follows:'. Where possible provide references to support your definitions.

Literature review

Unless you are writing a 'bare bones' type of research report where you are merely summarising the findings of a study, you will be expected to have familiarised yourself with other research in the same area. Because much of the justification of your methodology and discussion must be grounded on current literature you should be able to demonstrate a perspective on what the contemporary literature means in the context of your research. This requires undertaking a literature review.

Literature searching strategy

The first part of this section should comprise a description of how you collected your literature. For example: 'A review of the English language literature on …(insert subject area) was undertaken. Searches for publications on …(insert subject area) were made of Medline, The British Nursing Index, Social Services Abstracts, journals, books, papers from conferences, relevant national and international organisations, reference lists and any other form of relevant references that were encountered. For the Medline, Social Services Abstracts and British Nursing Index searches, the following terms were entered: … (insert search terms). Specific subject headings under which searches were made were: … (insert headings). The last electronic search was undertaken on …(insert date).'

Appraisal of literature

In the next part of the section you will need to make explicit how your review of key topic-based references in the literature provided further background to the study and how looking at the ways similar problems had been studied helped you to think about the approach that you took. You are also providing an argument to support the study that you undertook, based on what others had found and the interpretation of the key themes requiring further exploration through research. This will also enable you to account for how the study will help to build on current research and theory, fill gaps in existing knowledge or add to an area of knowledge and how the findings of your study will provide benefits to current practice or knowledge. The review of the related literature should also present a comprehensive development of the problem background.

Whether the review is in chronological or some other arrangement, it is imperative that the literature is critically analysed and is as current as possible, retaining a direct relevancy to the inquiry in hand. You need to appraise the literature, commenting on the overall quality and how far it goes towards addressing or informing the problem or area of interest. You need to evaluate the appropriateness of the design and process of the research in addition to merely the outcome (findings, conclusions) and comment on any perceived strengths and weaknesses of particular methods. Also, as mentioned in the previous chapter, the conclusions arrived at by the authors can be evaluated with regard to feasibility, validity and appropriateness, in this way possibly further justifying why you did your study.

Method

Study design

Here is the place to introduce your study design, which incorporates methods appropriate to answering the research question. You need to clearly describe the methods that you utilised and how the research was actually carried out. You also need to be able to justify the study design and express why the chosen methods are appropriate. For example, why a quantitative approach incorporating either a questionnaire survey or an experiment was relevant or, why a qualitative approach incorporating in-depth, unstructured interviews or focus group meetings was more appropriate.

You need to describe and explain:
● the key features of the research design
● the rationale for the choice of research paradigm and method

- the philosophical under-pinning of the approach
- how the chosen design links to existing literature in the topic area
- how you sought to reduce bias and/or enhance the credibility of findings
- how you considered the reliability and validity of the chosen methods
- how you considered any ethical issues raised
- whether statistical tests used in analysis of results were appropriate for the study and justified with respect to research literature.

With regard to the sample you used for your study you need to be able to clearly identify:

- from where the participants were recruited, or from where other data were found
- the sample size, giving justification for this number
- the sampling method that was used
- the characteristics that determined participant inclusion in or exclusion from the study
- where relevant, how participants were persuaded to take part, describing any incentive tactics, such as paying their expenses.

Ethical considerations

You are required to acknowledge that you have considered all ethical aspects of your study design and to state how you respond to or addressed these in carrying out your study. Particularly you need to demonstrate or describe:

- that approval was granted by the appropriate research ethics committee
- how participants' consent was obtained
- what the participants were told as to the nature of the study
- the steps taken to protect confidentiality or anonymity of the participants and data if relevant
- what will happen to the data once the research has been written up.

Research Instruments

Think of this part of the methods section as equivalent to the ingredients section of a recipe.

- List the research instruments used, such as: questionnaires, interview guides, focus group question prompts and include copies of all actual instruments in an appendix section.

- Describe the origin of each instrument (if the chosen instruments are based on a standardised source, provide full references and indicate if these sources have been adapted in any way, mentioning why and how and what risks of bias are recognised in adapting the tool).
- Describe the design, for example, how many question items, closed/open-ended questions and comment on validity and reliability issues.
- State if relevant, how the research instruments were piloted.
- Describe any equipment used, for example, machines for undertaking physiological measurements, tape recorders or diaries.

Data analysis

This is where you state how the data will be managed and analysed. This will include providing an outline of the statistical or qualitative methods that will be used, detailing stages of the analysis process. Note any computer programs that you plan to use, for example, MINITAB, EXCEL, SPSS, NUD*IST, ETHNOGRAPH, NVIVO.

A brief critique of the method that has been used may be included in the Method section and this can be discussed later with respect to the impact that the method may have had on the study as a whole.

Results

This section should comprise a clearly presented outline of the results, giving the results of the analysis but without any discussion or evaluation. This should be presented as succinctly and interestingly as possible. Use tables and graphs if appropriate. Any sample attrition should be described in full detail, that is, give a comprehensive description of all of those participants who did not complete the study and the reasons for non-completion.

Discussion

This is the section where an understanding is demonstrated of the implications of what has been found, in the context of contemporary thinking. A critical analysis of the methods used and the results, including the relationship between the results and other research should be evident. There should be a discussion as to what extent the study findings have adequately informed the research question or, if a hypothesis has been tested, whether the hypothesis is supported or rejected. Any limitations or weaknesses of the study should not be overlooked or hidden, for example, how any sample attrition has affected the study. There should be a description of how any problems encountered in the course of the study were dealt with. If appropriate, discuss how the findings from the study may improve upon previous research and how they may address any knowledge gap in the area. The discussion should be summarised by establishing the relevance and appropriateness of the outcomes and the meaning of the work with regard to the potential implications and value of the findings, in relation to the stated aim and objectives of the study and ultimately, to what extent the findings constitute knowledge to generate evidence to inform how practice can be improved.

Conclusion

The conclusion section should be a recapitulation of the study and its major components together with a summary of the principle findings. You should comment on the overall general-isability and applicability of the findings to the particular area of practice. This final section should present conclusions derived from the completion of the research, and the interpretation of the meanings and implications of the evidence. It is important that the evidence and conclusions are related to the literature reviewed. The conclusion should also include a presentation of recommendations for policy and/or practice and service delivery and for future research, listing possible areas and methods of inquiry.

References

References used in the text should be double-checked for accuracy and listed according to the system as required by the institute, organisation or journal to which the paper or report is being submitted.

Summary

This chapter has given a general overview of the requirements for research writing. As stated earlier, the above sections in this chapter are intended only as a general guide to research paper or research report writing and should not be seen as 'written in stone'. The techniques described are intended to be transferable to most types of research endeavour. The following chapter discusses research governance and ethics.

Chapter 11

Research governance and ethics

Introduction

Acquiring approval for a research study, from the necessary research governance department (usually from the research and development office of an organisation) and from the appropriate research ethics committee, is normally the last stage of the process of study design and preparation, that is, before the actual research begins 'for real'. However, the researcher should keep issues pertaining to research governance and research ethics at the forefront of their mind throughout the process of developing the research question or hypothesis and developing the study design. This is because if any potential problems arising from either research governance or research ethics are not considered then you may find that you have to completely redesign your study and that a lot of unnecessary hard work will have been undertaken in preparing a study that you have been prohibited from doing because it does not comply with research governance and/or research ethics committee requirements. This chapter gives an overview of what research governance and research ethics entail, including some information about the role of research ethics committees.

Research governance framework for health and social care

Research and development in health and social care is largely dependent on government funding and needs to have public confidence and support. Therefore it is essential that such research and development is conducted in accordance with regulations that are both stringent and transparent (Pierce 2007).

The UK government is committed to enhancing the contribution of research to health and social care. Research is seen as essential to the successful promotion and protection of health and well-being, and also to modern, effective health and social care services. However, it is recognised that research can involve an element of risk, both in terms of return on investment and sometimes for the safety and well-being of the research participants. Thus, appropriate governance of research is essential to ensure that the public can have confidence in and benefit from, quality research in health and social care. It is recognised that the public has a right to expect high scientific, ethical and financial standards, transparent decision-making processes, clear allocation of responsibilities and robust monitoring (DoH 2005).

The research governance framework applies to all research that is under the responsibility of the Secretary of State for Health. That is, research that is concerned with the protection and promotion of public health, research undertaken in or by the Department of Health, the NHS, and research undertaken by or within social care agencies. This includes clinical and non-clinical research, research that is undertaken by NHS, other health care or social care practitioners or staff, using the resources provided by health and social care organisations and institutions and universities within the health and social care systems that might have an impact on the quality of those services (DoH 2005).

The research governance framework is grounded on principles that apply generally to research in health and social care. It applies to the full range of research types, contexts and methods, to ensure that research across health and social care should consistently comply with the same general standards of governance (DoH 2005). The research governance framework is of direct relevance to all those who host, conduct, participate in, fund and manage health and social care research. It is not just for investigators, managers or any one professional group. All staff, regardless of position or seniority, have a role to play in the conduct of research (DoH 2005).

Research and Development (R&D) departments within organisations have the responsibility to apply the research governance framework. R&D departments must be aware of all research undertaken in their organisation, involving participants, organs, tissue or data obtained through the organisation. Also they are required to co-ordinate the research governance process and to ensure that any research projects will not have a negative impact on the organisation. It should be remembered that all research incurs some kind of cost and it is one of the purposes of R&D officers to ensure that these costs are balanced by the benefit of the research for the organisation. The R&D department also ensures that the organisation, or somebody within it, takes responsibility for any research and its conduct. R&D departments must also maintain a record of all research undertaken through or within the organisation (including research that students undertake as part of their training) in order to ensure that patients, patients' advocates, service users and carers, and care professionals are provided with information about any research that is likely to have a direct effect on their care, their experience of care, or their work within the organisation (DoH 2005).

Terminology box

Research governance
- Sets out principles, requirements and standards and defines mechanisms to deliver standards in the following domains: Ethics, Science, Information, Health, Safety and Employment, Finance and Intellectual Property
- Facilitates continuous improvement of standards
- Ensures monitoring and assessment arrangements
- Works towards reduction of unacceptable adverse incidents and variations in health and social care research practice
- Promotes good practice and quality in research, undertaken by appropriately qualified, skilled and experienced researchers
- Ensures effective use of professional judgement
- Prevents poor performance and misconduct
- Ensures ethical principles are adhered to.

Research issues in health and social care

There are powerful incentives to adhere to the principles, requirements and standards of good practice set out in the framework. These include the law, the duty of care in the NHS and social care, and the high professional and ethical standards that most care professionals and researchers uphold. Everyone involved in research with human participants, their organs, tissue or data is responsible for understanding and following the law and the principles of good practice relating to ethics, science, information, finance and health and safety, set out in the research governance framework (DoH 2005).

Mechanisms to monitor the quality of research, such as audit, inspection, risk management and regular staff appraisal procedures can assist in the monitoring of research governance. Coherent systems are required to monitor performance, to identify best practice and shortfalls, to enhance public confidence and help to prevent adverse events. It is an offence not to comply with the law for clinical trials involving medicines. For other research, those involved may be liable under common law if they are negligent. The Department of Health will work with its partners to develop coherent systems for monitoring research governance and addressing shortcomings (DoH 2005).

Research governance in social care

Research governance in social care

A core standard for health and social care organisations is that they have systems to ensure the principles and requirements of the research governance framework are consistently applied. While the same principles apply across health and social care research, the way in which the relevant standards are reached will be different according to the type of research undertaken, the particular context and the specific method or methods. For example, compared with much research in the NHS, research in social care may differ in scale, volume and funding, as well as in the mix of various stakeholders, the organisational context and the range of academic disciplines. The arrangements and mechanisms for implementing research governance in social care research are likely to have features that are particular to social care (DoH 2005).

Quality research culture

Quality research culture

The research governance framework seeks to promote what is described as a quality research culture (DoH 2005). The key elements of a quality research culture are as follows:

- respect for participants' dignity, rights, safety and well-being
- valuing the diversity within society
- personal and scientific integrity
- leadership
- consent sought according to ethical requirements
- honesty
- accountability
- active involvement of service users and carers
- openness – scientific review by independent experts, easy access to information on research, including to those who have participated
- clear and supportive management
- value for money
- recognition of intellectual property rights

(DoH 2005).

Research ethics

Research ethics

While the terms 'ethics' and 'morals' are often used interchangeably, it may be useful to see 'morals' as pertaining to personal values and beliefs based on our individual life experiences and 'ethics' as being in relation to professional values and philosophies (Terry 2007).

Historically, there have been incidents whereby vulnerable individuals or groups have been harmed by unethical research conduct (Stanley & McLaren 2007). These incidents have led to the development of codes of conduct and guidance along with requirements to undertake ethical reviews of proposed research which involves human participants (Stanley & McLaren 2007). With regard to research ethics in health and social care, the dignity, rights, safety and well-being of participants must be the primary consideration in any research study. Those undertaking research should be aware of and should respect the diversity of human conditions, of society and in particular the multicultural nature of society. Whenever relevant, researchers need to take into consideration age, disability, gender, sexual orientation, race, culture, ethnicity and religion in the design, undertaking and reporting of research studies (DoH 2005). Furthermore, research evidence that is made available to policy makers and others should reflect the diversity of the general population (DoH 2005).

All those involved in research also have an ethical duty to ensure that they, and those researchers they employ and manage are appropriately qualified, both by education and experience, for the role they play in relation to any research (DoH 2005). They must be aware of, and have ready access to sources of information and support in undertaking that role (DoH 2005). All existing sources of evidence, including systematic reviews, must be carefully considered before undertaking research. Research which unnecessarily duplicates other work or which is not of sufficient quality to usefully contribute something to existing knowledge, is deemed to be unethical (DoH 2005). Furthermore, all data that are collected must be handled and stored in compliance with the data protection act.

Informed consent

Informed consent

Informed consent is at the heart of ethical research and means that participants understand the potential risks of a study and all other aspects of what it involves. Participants must not be coerced in any way into taking part in a research study, this includes not telling potential participants everything they need to know about the study. After participants have been fully briefed about the study it is then necessary to check to ensure that they understand what has been explained to them. This is particularly important when recruiting people for clinical trials for the purpose of drug testing. Indeed, some research, such as clinical drug trials may involve a degree of risk of injury, pain or discomfort to those participating in it. For a study to be perceived as ethical, these risks, or adverse events must be kept to a minimum and always be in proportion to the potential benefits of such research studies (DoH 2005). As was indicated above, these risks must be fully explained to the partici-pants but also to the relevant research ethics committee. Furthermore, arrangements for any compensation in the event of adverse events occurring must be made explicit.

Research studies involving individuals need to have appropriate arrangements in place for obtaining informed consent, and the ethics review process pays particular attention to such arrange-ments. In addition, the law provides special protection for people who are unable to give consent on their own behalf. Thus, care is required when seeking to obtain consent from children (via their parents or guardians) and from vulnerable adults, for example, those who have mental health problems or learning difficulties. The Mental Capacity Act (2005) which came into force in 2007 provides safeguards for people who lack the capacity to consent to research. In obtaining informed consent it is necessary to ensure that relevant information about the study is provided in appropriate written, pictorial or other form and that the responsibilities of the researcher, the participants and any relatives, carers or supporters are clearly explained and fully understood (DoH 2005).

Newman *et al.* (2005) warn of some of the potential problems in recruiting people with learning difficulties into research studies involving social care, for example, the situation that may arise when having to end a research-based relationship with lonely or vulnerable people at the end of a study.

Also, under the Medicines for Human Use (Clinical Trials) Regulations 2004, specific conditions and principles apply to informed consent, and to the recruitment of minors and incapac-itated adults. There is a legal requirement for review by an appropriate body, usually a research ethics committee, and for researchers to follow a statutory Code of Practice in testing medicines on humans (DoH 2005).

It is recognised that participants or potential participants in research studies, and the public in general can also help to ensure that appropriate standards are understood and met (DoH 2005). It is also recognised that effective and responsive services are dependent on good quality research. Therefore, it is recommended that all those who use health and social care services should give serious consideration to becoming involved in developing or partic-ipating in research. In addition, it is increasingly being recognised that potential participants in research studies and those who may be affected by the outcome of the study, should wherever possible, be involved in the design, analysis and dissemination of such research.

Ethical dilemmas

Ethical
dilemmas

Parahoo (2006) notes that there are ethical implications at every stage of the research process. In fact, prior to research even taking place, a decision not to undertake research and continue to base practice on customs and traditions may be perceived as unethical in certain circumstances because this inaction may serve to deny service users the best possible care (Parahoo 2006). This is particularly so when a given service, the effectiveness of which is unproven, is provided to large numbers of people, because the service providers think that people will benefit from it (Newman *et al.* 2005). As was suggested in Chapter 2 by Haynes (2002), the evidence-based practice (EBP) movement has imparted something of a moral imperative whereby it is implied that practitioners should keep up to date with advances in practice and offer these to service users.

However, it was also suggested that this may lead to further unresolved ethical dilemmas in distributive justice. This is exemplified by the continuing ethical tension between the epidemiology-influenced, population-based, consequentialist ethos of providing the greatest good for the greatest number, which generates the majority of perceived best evidence that the advocates of EBP would like practitioners and patients to pay attention to, versus the deontological, individualistic ethos of medicine, that is, providing the best care possible for each individual patient, something which doctors are sworn to do (Haynes 2002). Haynes (2002) commented that a resolution to this ethical tension had not yet been found, in particular, the EBP movement had not even taken a clear stance on it.

In part echoing Haynes (2002), Parahoo (2006) perceived EBP as being population-based rather than individual-based, offering the greatest good for the greatest number, while individual needs may remain largely ignored. Thus, the ethical dilemma remains; given the escalating costs of health care, driven by newer diagnostic and therapeutic interventions, will the proceeds and resources of new science be fairly distributed (Haynes 2002)? It is apparent then that there are ethical dilemmas beyond the research process with regard to how we should best apply research-generated evidence and technology. Furthermore, given that it was not until fairly recently that professional journals insisted that authors provided information about obtaining research ethics committee approval for research that was being reported, we may ask if it is truly ethical to inform practice with evidence derived from any published study where it has not been made explicit that research ethics committee approval was acquired? It should be borne in mind that there are many 'landmark' papers in high quality, high impact journals which appear not to have met this requirement. These and other ethical dilemmas remain unresolved.

Terminology box

Research ethics
- Dignity, confidentiality, rights, safety and wellbeing of research participants are primary considerations
- Informed consent of participants is paramount
- Emphasis on the incorporation of beneficence, non-maleficence
- Independent ethical review required of all research involving service users, practitioners, volunteers, organs, tissue or data
- Where possible, participants should be involved in research design, analysis and dissemination
- Any risk to participants must always be minimised and clearly explained
- Respect for diversity of human culture and conditions.

Research issues in health and social care

Research ethics committees

**Research
ethics
committees**

The Department of Health requires that health and social care research involving patients, service users, care professionals or volunteers, or their organs, tissue or data, is reviewed independently to ensure it meets ethical standards (DoH 2005). Therefore, every proposal involving health and social care research must be subjected to review by experts in the relevant fields who are able to offer independent advice on the quality of such research (DoH 2005). Most often, this type of review is undertaken by a research ethics committee.

However, it should be noted that there are other mechanisms available for the process of peer review of proposed research studies. For example, researchers who are applying for funding from bodies such as the Economic and Social Research Council or the Medical Research Council will find that in order to be successful in obtaining funds, they must first have their proposal put through a rigorous peer review procedure, often entailing their proposal being reviewed by a series of peer reviewers and on several occasions. The procedure for peer review should be in proportion to the scale of the research and the risks involved. For example, in some circumstances, an external panel of independent experts may be invited to review a programme or a controversial or costly proposal (DoH 2005). In others, an organisation may invite established research teams to determine details of the elements of an overall programme of research which has been reviewed externally (DoH 2005). For student research projects, the university supervisor is normally able to provide adequate review (DoH 2005). If a research study, whatever the context, is to be considered as ethical, it is paramount that the interests of the research participants come first. Those who are responsible for this need to be satisfied that they have taken all reasonable steps to ensure that they are able to protect the dignity, rights, safety and the well-being of participants (DoH 2005).

However, even when research proposals have been independently peer reviewed, no research study within the NHS involving individuals, their organs, tissue or data can commence until it has approval from a research ethics committee. Research ethics committees are required to be independent when formulating advice with regard to the ethical implications of a proposed research study and ethics committee reviews must be impartial (DoH 2005). Thus, while they work in collaboration with those responsible for research governance, NHS research ethics committees are not part of the NHS Trust R&D management structures (DoH 2005). While they operate within a framework of standards and NHS management, neither the Department of Health nor NHS bodies are entitled to interfere with NHS research ethics committees decisions (DoH 2005). Research ethics committees' appointing authorities must have systems to appoint members and convene them, to seek recognition if the law requires it, and to support them and monitor their performance (DoH 2005). In addition, research ethics committees require researchers working in the NHS to keep them informed of the progress of a study. Research ethics committees are responsible for reviewing the ethical acceptability of a study and whether it should continue in the light of such information (DoH 2005).

In this way, research ethics committees provide an independent opinion, although the ultimate decision whether or not to grant permission for research to take place within a health care organisation rests with the R&D department (DoH 2005). Similarly, Directors of Social Services are responsible for considering permission for social care research conducted within their local authorities. However, subject to a favourable response from the research ethics committee, health and social care organisations do not generally withhold permission to undertake research approved by the ethics committee unless there are local factors that would result in an unacceptable impact on the quality of health or social care (DoH 2005).

It is not for research ethics committees or reviewers to give legal advice, nor are they liable for any of their decisions in this respect (DoH 2005). It is the researchers and the health or social care organisations who have the responsibility not to break the law (DoH 2005). If a research ethics committee suspects that a research proposal might contravene the law, the committee is expected to advise both the chief investigator and the appropriate authority (DoH 2005).

Research ethics committee review in social care

Despite the considerable symmetry between effective, appropriate interventions and ethical behaviour in social care practice (Newman *et al.* 2005), the arrangements and procedures for research ethics committee review in social care research are less well developed than in the area of health care. Indeed, there is no system which can be compared to the well-established NHS network of research governance offices and research ethics committees (DoH 2005). While options for ethics review of social care research are under consideration, for the time being, all those involved in social care research are advised to use their best endeavours to ensure that it is conducted to high ethical standards and wherever possible draw on existing arrangements for independent ethics review (DoH 2005). For example, many universities have research ethics committees that advise on the ethics of social care studies (DoH 2005). In addition, the Association of Directors of Social Services (ADSS) research group advises the ADSS and individual Directors and Social Services on the ethics, quality and relevance of proposals for multi-site studies (DoH 2005). Where these arrangements are not available or appropriate, the sponsor of the research study is expected to take responsibility for arranging an independent ethics review (DoH 2005).

Research ethics committees may decide not to grant approval for research study proposals for a whole range of reasons. For example, as was indicated earlier in this chapter, a study with inappropriate objectives or a design that cannot achieve the stated objectives will be deemed as a waste of time and resources and is therefore likely to be considered unethical (DoH 2005). However, given that the notion of informed consent is at the heart of ethical issues, one of the most common reasons for ethics committees not to approve a proposal or to ask for amendments is a poorly written participant information sheet with inadequate information and a poorly written consent participant form.

Summary

This chapter is not intended to be a definitive work on research governance or research ethics. These are vast subject areas in their own right and it would be possible to write a whole book on one or both areas, such as Leathard and McLaren (2007). Thus, the purpose of this chapter has been to highlight some of the salient points with regard to how these issues affect research and the importance of being aware of the need to obtain the appropriate regulatory approval early on in the process of planning and designing a piece of research. It is also apparent that there are ongoing developments with regard to the regulatory framework with regard to social care research and various ongoing ethical dilemmas concerning the distribution of resources and access to 'best' evidence-based care which the researcher may benefit from being aware of.

Chapter 12
Conclusion

The first chapter of this book comprised a brief historical journey to enable contemplation of some of the significant philosophers and thinkers who influenced knowledge construction and modern scientific development and whose concepts still underpin approaches to contemporary health and social care research. In contemplating the 'Scientific Revolution' and the march towards modernism, we saw how confidence in knowledge based on belief, metaphysics, divinity, superstition, spiritualism, intuition, faith, folklore and theological revelations has been gradually undermined by recognition of the need for empirical knowledge based on evidence generated through experience, reasoning (which may however include a degree of intuition), observation and experiment, namely, positivist, objective scientific 'truths', although these are tempered by a degree of scepticism. It was also noted though that knowledge based on religious faith, or for that matter, knowledge based on any other type of strong belief system, has not been superseded by contemporary scientific knowledge. Furthermore, there remain many uncertainties in the world today, some of which are represented by the dichotomies introduced in the first chapter which have served as themes and been revisited in various parts of the book. We have also seen that some of these uncertainties are more amenable to being addressed through research than others and some are more amenable to being addressed by particular types of research.

We have seen how the ethos of evidence-based practice (EBP) has proliferated in health and social care and despite the various shortcomings, criticisms and barriers, EBP is necessary if we are to provide clinically effective and cost-effective care to an increasing population. Indeed, the economics of health and social care resources is a major issue in contemporary society and for this reason alone, despite questions over the evidence for effectiveness of EBP and suggestions of EBP having ideological status, it is likely that EBP is here to stay.

We have looked at different types of research question and hypotheses and the relationship between practice, research, theory and the generation of knowledge that informs evidence to underpin EBP. It is apparent that while addressing the antithesis of knowledge, namely uncertainty, is a basic principle of scientific enquiry, it should be borne in mind that knowledge acquisition is not straightforward. Indeed, knowledge systems represent complex series of values, assumptions and methodological rules governing what might constitute appropriate knowledge in a given time and place. Therefore, in the pursuit of our research goals we need to contemplate the fact versus value dichotomy and consider that all knowledge is grounded in historical and social circumstances, remembering that values can be translated into 'scientific facts'. These 'facts' will then guide the research question or hypothesis that we decide upon, also the research approach and the methods that we utilise.

We have looked at quantitative research methods and analysis of quantitative, numerical data. We have seen how the findings of quantitative research may be used to predict outcomes, leading to the prevention of undesirable ones. Also quantitative research is useful in identifying trends, patterns, prevalence, attitudes, needs, roles, activities, satisfaction, beliefs, competence, service delivery and organisation, testing and evaluation of new interventions and/or comparing them with existing ones. It can inform policy decisions and justify expenditure. It is apparent that despite criticisms, quantitative research is valuable and important in health and social care and that quantitative research studies are still the favoured approach for those who provide funding for research and this is not likely to change in the near future. Thus, despite challenges from qualitative quarters in recent decades, since the introduction of EBP, quantitative research has gained a new impetus and has proliferated.

However, because problems faced by health and social care practitioners are never static and constantly changing, it is necessary to choose the research theory and approach that is best suited to solving the relevant problem. Thus, if we are dealing with subjective reality, as opposed to objective evidence, then qualitative research approaches are more appropriate and this is reflected in the increasing popularity of the use of qualitative research methods in health and social care.

Examining various qualitative research methods and analysis of qualitative data has provided insight as to how these methods are able to facilitate a more patient/client/service user-centred approach and a move away from traditional, positivist informed quantitative research approaches, which are typically based on the assumptions of the natural sciences. This has led to greater emphasis upon the uniqueness of the individual's understanding of the world which they inhabit and in particular, understanding of what it is like to experience illness and how people's lives may be changed by it.

We have considered the dichotomies between objectivity and subjectivity and between quantitative and qualitative research. Paradoxically, we have then considered that it may be reasonable for qualitative and quantitative approaches to complement each other and further that it is feasible to combine them. This is due to the complex and rapidly changing society (and world) we inhabit demanding that we need to innovate with existing theoretical assumptions and methods. Indeed it may be suggested that the qualitative versus quantitative debate is becoming increasingly anachronistic and irrelevant. Despite the two approaches being designed to answer different types of questions, they have been combined for a number of reasons, including meeting different needs at different stages of a project, or compensating for shortcomings in a particular method.

We have examined a number of checklist tools for critically appraising research evidence. Also, emphasis was placed on the fact that, in both developing research studies or in interpreting the findings of studies, the researcher's values are always at play. Furthermore, we must be wary of research findings written up by parties with vested interests as these are likely to contain overstatements, unsubstantiated connections or explanations, or results inappropriately generalised beyond the scope of the study.

We have looked at the general format and sequence for writing up research findings and how these may be presented.

Research issues in health and social care

With regard to research governance and research ethics, we have considered the importance of being aware of the need to obtain the appropriate regulatory approval early on in the process of planning and designing a piece of research and of the various ongoing ethical dilemmas concerning the distribution of resources and access to 'best' evidence-based care which the researcher may benefit from being aware of.

We have considered the important issue of terminology throughout this book, with terminology check boxes provided in various places. It is apparent though that there is a lack of agreement with regard to the terminology used to describe various concepts in health and social care research. Examples of this include the lack of agreement on what actually constitutes grounded theory as a research practice and lack of definition on what the process of triangulation is, as this appears to be used in a number of ways and contexts, sometimes consistently but sometimes with distinct differences.

Hopefully, though, in an increasingly research-conscious society where research generated, evidence-based practice proliferates, through reading this book the reader will have developed more of an enquiring, research orientated outlook to life in general but in particular, will have acquired a better grasp of many of the concepts and issues pertinent to contemporary health and social care research.

References

van den Akker, E.H., Hoes, A.W., Burton, M.J. & Schilder, A.G.M. (2004). 'Large international differences in adeno-tonsillectomy rates.' *Clinical Otorhinolaryngology* 29: 161–4.

Allgemeine Deutsche Biographie (1912) Leipzig, Germany: Bavarian Academy of Sciences.

Arride-Stirling, J. (2001). 'Thematic networks: an analytic tool for qualitative research.' *Qualitative Research* 1 (3): 385–405.

Bandolier (2007). http://www.medicine.ox.ac.uk/bandolier/booth/painpag/Acutrev/Analgesics/AP01 2.html (Accessed 23/10/08)

Berridge, V. (1999). *Opium and the People.* London: Free Association Books.

Bonnar, J. & Sheppard, B.L. (1996). 'Treatment of menorrhagia during menstruation: Randomised controlled trial of ethamsylate, mefenamic acid, and tranexamic acid.' *British Medical Journal* 313: 579–82.

Bradley, E.H., Curry, L.A. & Devers, K.J. (2007). 'Qualitative data analysis for health services research: developing taxonomy, themes, and theory.' *Health Services Research* 42(4):1758–72.

Brink, P. & Wood, M. (1994). *Basic Steps in Planning Nursing Research from Question to Proposal* (4th edn). London: Jones and Bartlett.

Broad, C.D. (1978). *Kant: An Introduction.* Cambridge: Cambridge University Press.

Bryman, A. (2004). *Social Research Methods.* 2nd Edition. UK: Oxford University Press.

Caine, C. & Kenrick, M. (1997). 'The role of clinical directorate managers in facilitating evidence-based practice: A report of an exploratory study.' *Journal of Nursing Management* 5, 157–65.

Centre for Appraisal Skills Programme (CASP) (2005) Available at http://www.phru.nhs.uk/Pages/PHD/CASP.htm Accessed 30/01/09.

Clarke, D. (2006). *Descartes: A Biography.* Cambridge: Cambridge University Press.

Closs, J. & Bryar, R.M. (2001). 'The BARRIERS Scale: Does it fit the current MHS research culture?' *Nursing Times Research* 6: 853–65.

Closs, S.J. & Cheater, F.M. (1999). 'Evidence for nursing practice: A clarification of the issues.' *Journal of Advanced Nursing* 30 (1): 10–17.

Colaizzi, P. (1978). 'Psychological research as the phenomenologist views it' in R. Valle and M. Kings (eds), *Existential Phenomenological Alternative for Psychology.* New York: Oxford University Press.

Cowan, D.T., Norman, I.J. & Coopamah, V.P. (2005). 'Competence in nursing practice: A controversial concept: A focussed review of literature.' *Nurse Education Today* 25: 355–62.

Cowan, D.T., Wilson-Barnett, J., Griffiths, P., Vaughan, D.J.A., Gondhia, A. & Allan, L.G. (2005). 'A randomised, double-blind, placebo-controlled, cross-over pilot study to assess the effects of long-term opioid drug consumption and subsequent abstinence in chronic non-cancer pain patients receiving controlled-release morphine.' *Pain Medicine* 6: 113–21.

Denzin, N.K. (1989). *The Research Act: A Theoretical Introduction to Sociological Methods*. Englewood Cliffs NJ: Prentice-Hall.

Denzin, N.K. & Lincoln, Y.S. (eds) (1994). *Handbook of Qualitative Research*. London: Sage Publications.

Department of Health (DoH) (2005). *Research Governance Framework for Health and Social Care* (1st edition March 2001, 2nd edition April 2005). London: Department of Health.

DePoy, E. & Gitlin, L.N. (1994). *Introduction to Research: Multiple Strategies for Health and Human Services*. Baltimore: Mosby.

Dixon-Woods, M., Agarwal, S., Jones, D., Young, B. & Sutton, A. (2005). 'Synthesising qualitative and quantitative evidence: a review of possible methods.' *Journal of Health Service Research Policy* 10 (1): 45–53.

Driver-Dunckley, E., Samanta, J. & Stacy, M. (2003). 'Pathological gambling associated with dopamine agonist therapy in Parkinson's Disease.' *Neurology* 61, pp. 422–3.

Dunn, J. (1984). *Locke: A Succinct Introduction*. Oxford: Oxford University Press.

Elstein, A.S. (2004). 'On the origins and development of evidence-based medicine and medical decision making.' *Inflammation Research*. 53 Supplement 2: S184–9.

Everitt, A. (2002), 'Research and development in social work', in Adams, R., Dominelli, L. and Payne, M. (eds), *Social Work, Themes, Issues and Critical Debates*, London: Palgrave in association with The Open University.

Fender, G.R., Prentice, A., Gorst, T., Nixon, R.M., Duffy, S.W., Day, N.E. & Smith, S.K. (1999). 'Randomised controlled trial of educational package on management of menorrhagia in primary care: the Anglia menorrhagia education study.' *British Medical Journal* 8 (318): 1246–50.

Feyerabend, P. (1975). *Against Method: Outline of an Anarchistic Theory of Knowledge*. London: New Left.

Foss, C. & Ellefsen, B. (2002). 'The value of combining qualitative and quantitative approaches in nursing research by means of method triangulation.' *Journal of Advanced Nursing* 40 (2): 242–8.

Foucault, M. (1972). *The Archaeology of Knowledge*. London: Tavistock.

Glaser, B. & Strauss, A. (1967). *The Discovery of Grounded Theory*. Chicago: Chicago Press.

Gordon, T. & Cameron, J.L. (2000). *Evidence-Based Surgery*. Hamilton, Canada: BC Decker.

Gossop, M. (2000). *Living with Drugs*. Aldershot, UK: Ashgate.

Grant, C., Gallier, L., Fahey, T., Pearson, N. & Sarangi, J. (2000). 'Management of menorrhagia in primary care.' *British Journal of Family Planning* 26: 227–8.

Greenhalgh, T. (1997a). 'How to read a paper: Statistics for the non-statistician I: Different types of data need different statistical tests.' *British Medical Journal* 315: 364–6.

References

Greenhalgh, T. (1997b). 'How to read a paper: Statistics for the non-statistician II: "Significant" relations and their pitfalls.' *British Medical Journal* 315: 422–5.

Greenhalgh, T. (1997c). 'How to read a paper: papers that report drug trials.' *British Medical Journal* 315: 480–83.

Greenhalgh, T. (1997d). 'How to read a paper: Papers that summarise other papers (systematic reviews and meta-analyses).' *British Medical Journal* 315: 672–5.

Greenhalgh, T. & Taylor, R. (1997). 'How to read a paper: Papers that go beyond numbers (qualitative research).' *British Medical Journal* 315: 740–43.

Grypdonck, M.H.F. (2006). 'Qualitative Health Research in the Era of Evidence-based Practice' Keynote Address: Eleventh Qualitative Health Research Conference. *Qualitative Health Research*, 16 (10): 1371–85.

Guyatt, G., Cairns, J., Churchill, D., Cook, D., *et al.* Evidence-based Medicine Working Group (1992). 'Evidence-based medicine: A new approach to teaching the practice of medicine.' *Journal of the American Medical Association* 268: 2420–5.

Havens, G.R. (1955). *The Age of Ideas*. New York: Holt.

Haynes, R.B. (2002). 'What kind of evidence is it that evidence-based medicine advocates want health care providers and consumers to pay attention to?' *BioMed Central Health Services Research* 2 (3): 1–7.

Heidegger, M. (1962). *Being and Time*. Oxford: Blackwell.

Husserl, E. (1962). *Ideas: General Introduction to Pure Phenomenology*. Trans. W.R. Boyce Gibson. New York USA: Collier.

Jadad, A. & Enkin, M.W. (2007). *Randomized Controlled Trials: Questions, Answers and Musings,* 2nd edition. London: Blackwell/BMJ Books.

Jadad, A.R., Moore, R.A., Carroll, D., Jenkinson, C., Reynolds, D.J.M., Gavaghan, D.J. & McQuay, H.J. (1996). 'Assessing the quality of reports of randomized clinical trials: Is blinding necessary?' *Controlled Clinical Trials* 17: 1–12.

Jones, R. (1995). 'Editorial: Why do qualitative research?' *British Medical Journal* 311: 2.

Kemp Smith, N. (1941). *The Philosophy of David Hume*. London: Macmillan.

Kimchi, J., Polivka, B. & Stevenson, J.S. (1991). 'Triangulation: operational definitions.' *Nursing Research* 40: 364–6.

Kinn, S. & Curzio, J. (2005). 'Integrating qualitative and quantitative research methods.' *Journal of Research in Nursing* 10 (3): 317–36.

Kuhn, T.S. (1970). *The Structure of Scientific Revolutions*. Chicago: University of Chicago Press.

Laudan, L. (1977). *Progress and its Problems: Towards a Theory of Scientific Growth*. Berkeley: University of California Press.

Leathard, A. & McLaren, S. (eds) (2007) *Ethics: Contemporary Challenges in Health and Social Care*. Bristol UK: Policy Press.

Leys, M. (2003). 'Health technology assessment. The contribution of qualitative research.' *International Journal of Technology Assessment* 19: 317–29.

Likert, R. (1932). 'A technique for the measurement of attitudes.' *Archives of Psychology* 140: 52.

Locke, J. (1841 [1690]). *An Essay Concerning Human Understanding*, 29th edn. London: T. Tegg & Co.

Lubell, Y., Reyburn, H., Mbakilwa, H., Mwangi, R., Chonya, S., & Whitty, C.J.M. (2008). 'The impact of response to the results of diagnostic tests for malaria: Cost-benefit analysis.' *British Medical Journal* 336 (7637): 202–5.

Marks, D.F. (2002). *Review into Perspectives on Evidence Based Practice*. Health Development Agency, Public Health Evidence Steering Group.

Masterman, M. (1970). 'The nature of a paradigm' in Lakatos, I. and Musgrave, A. (eds), *Criticism and the Growth of Knowledge*. Cambridge: Cambridge University Press.

McKenna, H. (1997). *Nursing Theories and Models*. London: Routledge.

Mental Capacity Act (2005) (Loss of Capacity During Research Project) (England) regulations 2007.
Available at http://www.opsi.gov.uk/si/si2007/pdf/uksi_20070679_en.pdf
Accessed 28/08/08.

Millenson, M.L. (1997). *Demanding Medical Excellence. Doctors and Accountability in the Information Age.* Chicago: University of Chicago Press.

Miller, N.F. (1946). 'Hysterectomy: Therapeutic necessity or surgical racket?' *American Journal of Obstetrics and Gynaecology* 51: 804–10.

Newman, T., Moseley, A., Tierney, S. & Ellis, A. (2005). *Evidence-based Social Work: A Guide for the Perplexed*. Lyme Regis UK: Russell House.

Newton, I. (1803). *The Mathematical Principles of Natural Philosophy*. Trans. A. Motte. London: H.D. Symonds.

National Institute for Health and Clinical Excellence (NICE) (2007).
Available at http://www.nice.org.uk/ Accessed 23/01/07.

Omar, R. (2006). Meta Analysis and Systematic reviews. Practical Statistics for Medical Research, Dept of Statistical Science and UCL, Med stats unit. UCLH.

Open University (1991). *Medical Knowledge, Doubt and Uncertainty*. London: Open University.

Parahoo, K. (2006). *Nursing Research: Principles, Process and Issues*. 2nd edition. Basingstoke: Palgrave.

Petticrew, M. & Roberts, H. (2003). 'Evidence, hierarchies, and typologies: horses for courses.' *Journal of Epidemiology and Community Health* 57: 527–9.

Pierce, E. (2007). 'Ethics: Research governance for health and social care research' in Leathard, A. and McLaren, S. (eds) *Ethics: Contemporary Challenges in Health and Social Care*. Bristol UK: Policy Press.

Powers, B.A. & Knapp, T.R. (1995). *A Dictionary of Nursing Theory and Research*. 2nd edition. New York: Springer Publications.

Priest, H., Roberts, P. & Woods, L. (2002). 'An overview of three different approaches to the interpretation of qualitative data. Part 1: Theoretical issues.' *Nurse Researcher* 10 (1): 30–42.

Rawcliffe, C. (1995). *Medicine and Society in Later Medieval England*. Stroud: Sutton Publishing.

Robson, C. (2002) *Real World Research: A Resource for Social Scientists and Practitioners*. 2nd edition.Oxford, UK: Blackwell.

Rosen, E. (1995). *Copernicus and his Successors*. London: Hambledon Press.

Sackett, D.L. (1996). 'Evidence-based medicine: What it is and what it isn't.' *British Medical Journal* 312: 71–2.

Sandelowski, M. (1993). 'Theory unmasked, the uses and guises of theory in qualitative research.' *Research in Nursing and Health* 16: 213–18.

Sapsford, R. (1999). *Survey Research*. London: Sage Publications.

Savage, J. (2000). 'Ethnography and health care.' *British Medical Journal* 321: 1400–1402.

Schaler, J. (2000). *Addiction is a Choice*. Chicago: Open Court Publishing.

Sehon, S.R. & Stanley, D.E. (2003). 'A philosophical analysis of the evidence-based medicine debate.' *BioMed Central Health Services Research* 3 (14): 1–10.

Sharratt, M. (1996). *Galileo: Decisive Innovator*. Cambridge: Cambridge University Press.

Shih Fu Jin (1998). 'Triangulation in nursing research: issues of conceptual clarity and purpose.' *Journal of Advanced Nursing* 28 (3): 631–41.

Smith, M.J. (1998). *Social Science in Question*. London: Open University.

Social Care Institute for Excellence (SCIE) (2005). *Using knowledge in social care: Report 10. Developing the evidence-base for social work and social care practice*. Bristol: Policy Press.

Social Care Institute for Excellence (SCIE) (2007)
Available at http://www.scie.org.uk/ Accessed 23/01/07.

Stern, P.N. (1980). 'Grounded theory methodology: its uses and processes.' *Image* 12 (1): 20–33.

Stanley, R. & McLaren S. (2007). 'Ethical issues in health and social care research' in Leathard, A. and McLaren, S. (eds) *Ethics: Contemporary Challenges in Health and Social Care*. Bristol UK: Policy Press.

Strauss, A. (1987). *Qualitative Analysis for Social Scientists*. Cambridge: Cambridge University Press.

Strauss, A. & Corbin, J. (1998). *Basics of Qualitative Research: Grounded Theory Procedures and Techniques*. 2nd edition. London: Sage.

Terry, L. (2007). 'Ethics and contemporary challenges in health and social care' in Leathard, A. and McLaren, S. (eds) *Ethics: Contemporary Challenges in Health and Social Care*. Bristol UK: Policy Press.

Tiner, J.H. (1975). *Isaac Newton: Inventor, Scientist and Teacher*. Milford, Michigan: Mott Media.

Urbach, P. (1987). *Francis Bacon's Philosophy of Science*. La Salle IL: Open Court Publishing.

Van Kamm, A. (1966). *Existential Foundations of Psychology*. Pittsburgh: Duquesne University Press.

Weber, R.P. (1983). 'Measurement models for content analysis.' *Quality and Quantity* 17: 127–49.

White, R. & Taylor, S. (2002). 'Nursing practice should be informed by the best available evidence, but should first level nurses be competent at research appraisal and utilisation.' *Nurse Education Today* 22: 220–24.

Research issues in health and social care

Wilde, V. (1992). 'Controversial hypotheses on the relationship between researcher and informant in qualitative research.' *Journal of Advanced Nursing* 17: 234–42.

World Health Organisation (WHO) (1992). *International statistical classification of diseases and related health problems. 10th Revision*, Volume 1 (WHO-ICD-10). Geneva: World Health Organisation.

Wright, R.C. (1969) 'Hysterectomy, past present and future.' *Obstetrics and Gynaecology* 33: 360–63.

Yates, S. (1998). *The Challenge of Social Sciences: Issues in Social Research.* Milton Keynes: Open University.

Youngblut, J.M. & Brooten, D. (2001). 'Evidence-based nursing practice: Why is it important?' *AACN Clinical Issues* 4: 468–76.

http://www.statsdirect.com/try.htm Accessed 30/01/09

Index